HERALDS OF GOD

HERALDS
OF GOD

JAMES S. STEWART

How are they to believe in One of whom
they have not heard ? And how are they
ever to hear, without a herald ? And how
can men be heralds, unless they are sent
by God ?

St. Paul to the Romans

BAKER BOOK HOUSE
Grand Rapids, Michigan

Reprinted 1972 by
Baker Book House Company
from the original edition
copyrighted 1946 by
Hodder and Stoughton, Ltd.
London
Printed in the United States of America
ISBN: 0-8010-7976-4

Fifth printing, July 1979

To
ROSAMUND
ROBIN and JACK

PREFACE

I HAVE chosen the title of this book to stress one
fundamental fact, namely, that preaching exists,
not for the propagating of views, opinions and ideals,
but for the proclamation of the mighty acts of God.
This is demonstrably the New Testament conception
of the preacher's task; and it is this that will always
give preaching a basic and essential place at the very
heart of Christian worship.

To write about preaching is therefore to deal with
an enterprise with which not only the man in the pulpit
but the whole worshipping community is vitally and
intimately concerned: a fact which emboldens me to
hope that the pages which follow, addressed originally
as Lectures in the Universities of Edinburgh and
St. Andrews to Divinity students and ministers, will
have something to say to the wider circle of those who
Sunday by Sunday are hearers of the Word of God,
"loving the habitation of His house and the place
where His honour dwelleth," and perhaps even to
the critic in the back pew.

I desire here to record my thanks to the Trustees
of the Warrack Lectureship, for their invitation to

me to undertake this task, and to my friend, the Rev. Graham W. Hardy, B.D., who has revised the proofs.

James S. Stewart

North Morningside Church
Edinburgh

CONTENTS

		PAGE
PREFACE	. . . .	5
I. THE PREACHER'S WORLD	. . . .	9
II. THE PREACHER'S THEME	. . . .	58
III. THE PREACHER'S STUDY	. . . .	100
IV. THE PREACHER'S TECHNIQUE	. . .	141
V. THE PREACHER'S INNER LIFE	. . .	190

Chapter I

THE PREACHER'S WORLD

There shall always be the Church and the World
And the Heart of Man
Shivering and fluttering between them, choosing and chosen,
Valiant, ignoble, dark, and full of light
Swinging between Hell Gate and Heaven Gate.
And the Gates of Hell shall not prevail.
Darkness now, then
            Light.   T. S. Eliot, *The Rock*.

AMONG the tributes paid to the memory of Sir Walford Davies, one of the noblest was that of a brother musician, Dr. Vaughan Williams. He dwelt on the sacrifice which Walford Davies had chosen to make quite deliberately—the sacrifice of the more aloof, self-centred life of the composer, for that of the organizer, the advocate, the musical propagandist, the educator of popular taste and opinion; and then he added: "It is an eternal problem that confronts all those who feel they have the creative impulse—'shall I shut myself up from the world and follow the dictates of my artistic conscience, or shall I go down to the world of men and show them what I have learnt about eternity and beauty?' Walford Davies had no doubts—he was a born preacher and he determined to go and preach to the Gentiles. This decision," declared Vaughan Williams, "was probably right." I

9

fancy that no one who knows what Walford Davies did for music in this generation will dispute that verdict.

Now the same problem, the same critical decision to which Vaughan Williams called attention in the realm of creative art, reappears even more forcibly in religion; and here it is a problem, not for the few who possess the elusive quality of genius, but for the whole company of believers. "Shall I, as a Christian, be content to pursue the religious quest as a private hobby, and to develop my own spiritual life; or shall I concern myself personally for those outside, and take upon my heart deliberately the whole world's need for Christ?" No man, with the New Testament in his hand, can have a moment's hesitation about the answer. "What I live by," declared St. Augustine, "I impart."

You have decided this matter in the most emphatic way of all, putting your life itself into the decision. Or rather, it has been decided for you, by the constraint of a higher will. For you the issue has been settled. To bring men face to face with Christ has seemed to you a matter of such immense and overruling urgency that you propose to devote your whole life to doing nothing else. You are determined, God helping you, to go down to the world of men, and show them what you have learnt—what indeed you shall go on learning more clearly every day you live— about the eternity of redeeming love and the beauty of the Lord.

It is a thrilling, noble enterprise. It demands and deserves every atom of a man's being in uttermost self-commitment.

"To go down to the world of men." That thrusts upon us this crucial fact—that our work as preachers has to be done in the actual setting of a contemporary situation.

The Gospel, it is true, stands unchanged from age to age. It remains yesterday, to-day, and for ever the same. In the twentieth century, it is the identical message which was sent by the Lord to former generations through the mouths of His servants Spurgeon and Wesley and Latimer and Xavier and Chrysostom and the apostles. No protean fashions of thought can alter it. No ebb and flow of the tides of history can prevail to modify it. It is as immutable as God Himself.

But while the basic message thus remains constant and invariable, our presentation of it must take account of, and be largely conditioned by, the actual world on which our eyes look out to-day. The Gospel is not for an age, but for all time: yet it is precisely the particular age—this historic hour and none other—to which we are commissioned by God to speak. It is against the background of the contemporary situation that we have to reinterpret the Gospel once for all delivered to the saints; and it is within the framework of current hopes and fears that we have to show the commanding relevance of Jesus.

This is not a plea for so-called "topical" sermons. It is deplorable that God's hungry sheep, hoping for the pasture of the living Word, should be fed on disquisitions on the themes of the latest headlines. It is calamitous that men and women, coming up to the church on a Sunday — with God only knows what cares and sorrows, what hopes and shadowed memories, what heroic aspirations and moods of shame burdening their hearts—should be offered nothing better for their sustenance than one more dreary diagnosis of the crisis of the hour.

But this is not to say that the preacher must stand aloof, cultivating a spirit of detachment from the march of events. "What is history," cried Cromwell, "but God's unfolding of Himself?"—and the real work of the ministry in this generation will not be done by any man who shuts himself in with his academic interests and doctrinal theorizings, as though there were no surge and thunder of world-shattering events beating at his door. Surely in this immensely critical hour, when millions of human hearts are besieged by fierce perplexities; when so many established landmarks of the spirit are gone, old securities wrecked, familiar ways and habits, plans and preconceptions, banished never to return; when the soul is destined to meet, amid the crash of old beliefs, the ruthless challenge and assault of doubt and disillusionment; when history itself is being cleft in twain, and no man can forecast the shape of things to come—the Church needs men who, knowing the world around them, and knowing the Christ above them and within, will set the trumpet of the Gospel to their lips, and proclaim His sovereignty and all-sufficiency.

The question, therefore, is this: If the Gospel, in itself unchanging, must always be set forth in the nexus of a particular historical situation, what are the characteristic moods and tendencies which must influence the presentation of the message to-day?

Attempts are sometimes made to define the spirit of the age in a single phrase—to call it, for example, "an age of doubt," "an age of rationalism," "an age of revolt," and so on. But all such generalizations are misleading. The reality cannot be thus simplified. We have to reckon with a mental and spiritual climate full of the most baffling contradictions. It would indeed be true to say that the most characteristic feature of the modern mood is precisely the unresolved tension between opposing forces. Here we touch the very nerve of the preacher's problem. There are three directions in which this element of tension, of radical paradox and spiritual conflict, of thrust and counter-thrust, is manifesting itself dramatically in the world we face to-day.

I

First, there is the tension between *Disillusionment and Hope*.

You are going out with the evangel into a world which has reacted strongly and even violently against the bland humanistic optimism which dominated the opening decade of the century. Then the great watch-words were the adequacy of materialism, the inevit-ability of progress, and the sufficiency of man. Science, having finally broken through the bondage of ignor-ance, and having shattered the tyranny of superstition, was hailed as the New Messiah, the supreme disposer of human destiny. Indeed, so startling and spectacular were the boons and bestowals of this new Messianic age, so strange and exciting the faculties put at man's disposal, that one sinister fact went almost unobserved: all its gifts were double-edged. The dazzling splen-dours of its achievements masked only too effectively the grim truth—later to be learnt at an immeasurable cost of blood and tears—that science (to quote the words of Reinhold Niebuhr) "can sharpen the fangs of ferocity as much as it can alleviate human pain." That aspect was conveniently ignored. With this new Messiah leading the way, it was argued, was there any limit to what humanity might accomplish? It was an intoxicating prospect. Would not social effort, rein-forced by all the resources of technology, speedily bring the New Jerusalem down to earth from heaven? Surely the wilderness wanderings of the children of men were over, and the path of progress must now lead straight and unbroken to the shining Utopia of their dreams. The Renaissance humanists and the ancient sophists had been perfectly right: man was indeed the measure of all things. His will was the architect of destiny. His intelligence, storming the secrets of the universe, had occupied the throne of God.

"Thou art smitten, thou God," shouted Swinburne
vociferously,

> thou art smitten; thy death is upon thee, O Lord.
> And the love-song of earth as thou diest resounds through
> the wind of her wings—
> Glory to Man in the highest! for Man is the master of
> things.

Now it was hardly to be expected that in the heyday
of this confident utopianism religion could remain
uninfluenced and immune. The Bible might insist
that "your adversary the devil, as a roaring lion,
walketh about, seeking whom he may devour," but
theological liberalism smiled to itself in a superior and
even contemptuous way: it was not going to take such
rhetoric too seriously. The conceptions of the world
as fallen, of human nature as infected with a radical
taint, of sin as a vicious circle which could be broken
through only by supernatural action from outside—
these were classed as outmoded fictions, and relegated
to the scrap-heap of an antiquated theology. The
evolutionary hypothesis, so fruitful in other fields,
began to invade the deepest sanctities of the soul: it
now appeared that all man had to do for his redemption
was to

> Move upward, working out the beast,
> And let the ape and tiger die.

The Kingdom of Heaven was not, as Jesus and the
apostles had proclaimed it, a gift of God breaking into
history from the beyond: it was a human achievement,

the product of social amelioration, culture and scientific planning. Jesus Himself, according to this view, was the Pioneer of progress, the supreme Leader, the apex of the vanguard of the pilgrim host of humanity —not a terrific Being shattering history with the explosive word, "Before Abraham was, I am." Christianity sounded in men's ears as good advice, rather than good news: an exhortation to be up and doing, to fight the good fight and follow the gleam, not the announcement of something which God had already done, decisively and for ever. There was accordingly an inclination to regard the preacher as the purveyor of religious homilies and ethical uplift, not the herald of the mighty acts of God. So far did the prevailing mood push the tendency to "change the glory of the uncorruptible God into the image of corruptible man" that there actually appeared a plagiarizing hymn, "Nearer, Mankind, to thee, Nearer to thee": a sentiment, said G. K. Chesterton tersely if somewhat scurrilously, which "always suggested to me the sensations of a strap-hanger during a crush on the Tube." Characteristic of this whole attitude was the reduced emphasis upon a theology of atonement and redemption. Why should man, conscious as never before in history of his own vast potential resources, grovel as a miserable sinner, or confess himself immeasurably indebted to sheer unmerited grace?

> Every virtue we possess,
> And every victory won,
> And every thought of holiness

were—not "His alone," emphatically not that—our personal meritorious achievement, the praiseworthy product of our innate spirituality. It was a mood which came dangerously near to making religion itself the handmaid and confederate of that pride which is the final blasphemy and the basic sin of man.

To-day the scene is changed. When you go forth as preachers bearing Christ's commission, it is to a generation which has very largely repudiated the confident optimism of its predecessors. The great tower of Babel—collective man's *monumentum aere perennius* —has crashed, and the world is littered with the wreckage of disillusionment.

Back in 1918, a few days after the signing of the Armistice, Lord Curzon, moving the Address in the House of Lords, quoted the chorus from Shelley's *Hellas*:

> The world's great age begins anew,
> The golden years return.

Such sanguine words sound almost sardonic now. "We are living," confessed Aldous Huxley, "in a rather grisly morning-after." The shining dream has proved to be a mirage. Of what profit is man's creative power, theme of his proudest boasts, if it is to become by a strange irony of fate the very instrument of his self-destruction? The old, ruthless dilemma, to which St. Paul gave classic expression in the seventh of Romans, has man in its torturing grip. And across the human scene to-day there echoes the haunting, unbearably poignant cry of Jeremiah long ago: "The

17

harvest is past, the summer is ended, and we are not saved."

Along with this, there has crept a deeper note into theology. We are no longer inclined to underestimate the radical stubbornness of sin. It has been borne in upon us that human wisdom cannot solve the dark enigma, nor can human action break the fast-bound fetters of the world. If there is any healing for humanity's hurt, it must come, not from man's side, but from God's.

There is, however, a danger here. It is possible for the reaction from the creed of human self-reliance to be so violent that the disillusioned spirit is carried by it right across into pessimism and despair. Dark suspicions rear their heads. Has faith been a ghastly mistake? Is there perhaps no rationality anywhere? What if the spiritual interpretation of life is nothing more than the creation of pious sentiment, muddled thinking and credulity? How can the Christian evangel be relevant in a blatantly non-Christian world? Do not its basic axioms look frightfully incongruous and inapposite? Never forget as preachers that all around you to-day are men baffled and tormented by the assault of that fierce ultimate doubt.

I would have you notice, moreover, that theology itself, in certain of its aspects, has shared in the pessimistic reaction. There are those, for example, whose reflections on the contemporary scene have landed them in hopeless dualism. The world, as they see it, is the battleground where dark demonic forces wage war unceasingly with the hosts of heaven. By this conflict God Himself is limited, thwarted in His purposes, constrained to strive and struggle indecisively for the realization of His holy will. It is a recrudescence of the Manichaean heresy. It is quite oblivious of the repeated trumpet-note of the New Testament—that at the Cross once for all Christ raided the dark empire of evil, and vanquished the demons, and led captivity captive.

With others, again, the pessimistic mood expresses itself in religious quietism. They have carried their distrust of human nature to the point of denying the worth of any social action. Confronted with the collapse of the humanist gospel of man's self-redeemability, they seek refuge in the unethical mysticism of a thoroughgoing otherworldliness: "Oh that I had wings like a dove! for then would I fly away, and be at rest."

Once again, there are those for whom the pressure of disillusionment has resulted in theological irrationalism. Man, according to this view, is so radically corrupt that there is no point of his nature left at which the living God can take hold. If ever he was made in the divine image, so completely has that image been obliterated that to talk of fellowship between man and his Creator is downright sophistry and self-deception. The light of reason itself is treacherous and perfidious. He that would frame dogmas, let him abjure the aid of logic. He that glorieth, let him glory in his irrationalism! It is hard to believe that this position, supported though it is by great and honoured names, can maintain itself indefinitely. God intends His pilgrims to struggle through the Slough of Despond, not to make it their theological home.

Here let me interpolate a quite personal remark. If you as preachers would speak a bracing, reinforcing word to the need of the age, there must be no place for the disillusioned mood in your own life. Like your Master, you will have meat to eat that the world knows not of; and that spiritual sustenance, in so far as you partake of it daily, will strengthen your powers of resistance to the dangerous infection. Surely there are few figures so pitiable as the disillusioned minister of the Gospel. High hopes once cheered him on his way: but now the indifference and the recalcitrance of the world, the lack of striking visible results, the discovery of the appalling pettiness and spite and touchiness and complacency which can lodge in narrow hearts, the feeling of personal futility—all these have seared his soul. No longer does the zeal of God's House devour him. No longer does he mount the pulpit steps in thrilled expectancy that Jesus Christ will come amongst His folk that day, travelling in the greatness of His strength, mighty to save. Dully and drearily he speaks now about what once seemed to him the most dramatic tidings in the world. The edge and verve and passion of the message of divine forgiveness, the exultant, lyrical assurance of the presence of the risen Lord, the amazement of supernatural grace, the urge to cry "Woe is me if I preach not the Gospel" —all have gone. The man has lost heart. He is

20

disillusioned. And that, for an ambassador of Christ, is tragedy.

How to maintain yourselves against the menace of this mood—that I shall speak of more specifically when we come to consider the preacher's inner life. But maintain yourselves you must: or else—don't try to speak to men in the name of God! For your task is to confront the rampant disillusionment of the day, and smash it with the Cross of Christ and shame it with the splendour of the Resurrection. What makes your calling in the Church so urgent and so critical is the fact that human hearts, bombarded with grim perplexities and damaging shadows of despair, are crying as never before, "Is there any word from the Lord?" Men who have seen war's scourge let loose twice in a generation are not going to be put off with polite trivialities and polished essays and pulpit dialectic. They don't want our views, opinions, advice or arguments. *Is there any word from the Lord?* Tell us that, they demand. Has Christianity failed? Must God's hopes be wrecked for ever on the rock of man's anarchic nature? Are we mad to pray "Thy kingdom come"? These demonic forces of evil in the universe, mocking all our dreams and best endeavours—are they fated to have the last word? It is all very well to stand up in church and sing:

> So be it, Lord! Thy throne shall never,
> Like earth's proud empires, pass away;
> Thy Kingdom stands and grows for ever,
> Till all Thy creatures own Thy sway.

21

But is that true? What if it is only a pose, the silly pretence of the self-deceiving? Was Thomas Hardy perhaps right when he recommended Christianity to "throw up the sponge and say 'I am beaten,' and let another religion take its place"? There is the vast, intolerable mystery of suffering. Is there any word from the Lord about that? There is the more intimate and personal disillusionment, the monotonous misery of defeat in a man's own soul: "the good that I would, I do not; but the evil which I would not, that I do. O wretched man that I am!" Is there any word from the Lord about that? Such is the demand which thrusts itself clamorously and uncompromisingly upon the Church to-day. And to that demand, you—please God—shall have a right to speak.

Let me at this point remind you, for your encouragement, that if there is a vast amount of disillusionment going about in the world to-day, there is also an immense stirring of eager and passionate hope. The tension between these two attitudes is indeed one of the cardinal factors in the situation. Nor is this strange blending of disillusionment and hope in the minds of men so paradoxical as at first sight it may appear. For a complete breakdown of humanist self-confidence is a true *praeparatio evangelica*: it makes straight through the desert a highway for our God. Preach to a soul strong in untroubled egotism, *mens sibi conscia recti*—and it will be like hammering at granite. But bring the Gospel to bear upon a soul whose self-trust has been broken, and there before your very eyes the ancient miracle may be renewed, and the glory of the Lord be revealed. Complacence of any kind—whether it be national or social, intellectual or moral, humanitarian or religious—is God's greatest enemy. But when the foundations are undermined, and the edifice of man's vaunted achievements comes down with a crash, then is the time, declared Jesus, to "look up, and lift up your heads; for redemption draweth nigh."

Thus the very disillusionment of to-day is the raw material of the Christian hope. Men are beginning to suspect that no new order which seeks to erect itself on the ruins of the old can have one atom of survival-value, or be other than a patchwork and a sham, unless it has direct and deliberate reference to the mind and programme of God for humanity. Consider in this connection the following verdict, which comes significantly from Dr. C. E. M. Joad: "There is in many Englishmen to-day, and especially in young people newly come to maturity, a renewed interest in the religious view of the world, and a disposition to examine afresh, in the light of it, the traditional answers to fundamental questions which Christianity has provided. . . . That the seeds of a spiritual revival are germinating in the minds of the people of this country, I, for one, do not doubt." The fact is that to-day, as so often in past history, the very complexity of the human predicament becomes in Christ's hands a weapon for the further advance of His Kingdom. And

23

if your calling as preachers in this generation is one of immense difficulty, you will be strong in hope, giving glory to God, not in spite of the difficulties, but precisely because of them. For still to-day, as at the first, it is when the doors are shut, in the bitter hour of disillusionment, that Christ is apt to break in, and stand in the midst, and say "Peace be unto you." And then, out of the dark misery of self-despair, men begin to arise and shine, knowing that their light is come!

Don't listen to the lugubrious voices that incessantly deplore the deadness of the age, and groan about the thankless uphill task of the Christian ministry and the desolating lack of response. It is a thrilling hour in which to bear the commission of your Lord.

I find certain words of St. Paul to the Romans dramatically relevant here. The eighth chapter is one of the most lyrical and triumphant things that ever came from the heart of man: but the note of disillusionment is there. "To this day," wrote the apostle, "the entire creation sighs and throbs with pain." For none knew better than he that the shining civilization was demon-ridden, and that ruthless forces held the souls of men in bitter thraldom. But what his piercing insight saw was this, that the mood of tragic desperation was itself the harbinger of hope. Just because this sighing, groaning creation was racked with pain, it was also tense with a breathless expectancy:

> Still nursing the unconquerable hope,
> Still clutching the inviolable shade.

"The whole creation," wrote Paul, "waits with eager longing for the sons of God to be revealed." It is listening for the sound of a distant pilgrim chorus, the march of a great consecrated brotherhood in Christ, the decisive emergence of a new race, the true sons of God, sealed with the Cross. It is scanning the roads down which that ransomed host, that nobler breed of saints, shall come at destiny's hour to bring history to its fulfilment.

It is a daring, magnificent conception. Are we wrong to see in it a parable of that thrust and counter-thrust of disillusionment and hope upon which we look out to-day, and with which as preachers we have to reckon? When a generation has been robbed of its familiar gods of material security, progress, human self-sufficiency, or when the individual soul has found its conventional religion stolen away by the marauding forces of agnosticism, trouble and despair, then strikes God's hour to break in with His salvation. Must we not say that any weariness, unsettlement or consternation is in the last resort a blessed thing if it makes a man or an age in the mood to welcome God? It is a great thing to be brought right down to the depths, if so be that there at last we strike that bedrock which is the Rock of ages; a great thing that life itself should break up even violently the hard core of our proud self-reliance, if so be that the human spirit may be ready then to cast itself upon its ultimate resource in Jesus Christ.

Therefore I counsel you—let no fog of spiritual

defeatism chill your ministry. Refuse to listen to the lying voices which insinuate that this is an unpropitious hour for the proclamation of the faith. You are to be the heralds of a religion which once saw the blackest, most desperately unpropitious hour in history —the hour of the crucifying of Jesus—turned into history's crowning glory and mankind's brightest hope. Go forth, then, in the heartening assurance that this present cataclysmic hour is alive with spiritual potentialities.

To take but one striking line of evidence, there is the new demand, particularly amongst youth, for a cause worthy of sacrifice or devotion, the new urge towards complete self-commitment. It will be tragic if the Church cannot take that generous impulse and baptize it into Christ. If you are wise, you will not in your preaching mask or minimize the overwhelming, absolute nature of Christ's demand. Men are ready for a Leader who will unhesitatingly claim the last ounce of His followers' courage and fidelity. Field-Marshal Wavell has told, in his notable lectures entitled *Generals and Generalship*, the story of how Napoleon, when an artillery officer at the siege of Toulon, built a battery in such an exposed position that he was told he would never find men to man it. But Napoleon had a sure instinct for what was required. He put up a placard—"The battery of men without fear": and it was always manned. This is no time to be offering a reduced, milk-and-water religion. Far too often the world has been presented with a mild and undemanding half-Christianity. The Gospel has been emasculated long enough. Preach Christ to-day in the total challenge of His high, imperious claim. Some will be scared, and some offended: but some, and they the most worth winning, will kneel in homage at His feet.

II

I pass on now to a second form in which the fact of tension, of paradox and conflict—so characteristic, as we have remarked, of the mental and spiritual climate of to-day—thrusts itself upon the preacher of the Word. This is the radical tension between *Escapism and Realism*. You will encounter nothing more baffling than the way in which an urgent quest for reality and an intense desire to avoid reality at all costs can apparently consort together.

Consider the latter tendency first. Some of you will know St. John Adcock's striking poem *The Divine Tragedy*. It is an imaginative attempt to conceive what would happen if Jesus of Nazareth were to come back to the modern world; if some of those who profess our holy religion, and remain safe and snug behind a façade of second-hand dogma and devotion, were suddenly confronted with the blazing reality of Christ Himself. Hear the poet's conclusion:

> When a blithe infant, lapt in careless joy,
> Sports with a woollen lion—if the toy
> Should come to life, the child, so direly crost,
> Faced with this Actuality were lost. . . .

Leave us our toys, then; happier we shall stay
While they remain but toys, and we can play
With them and do with them as suits us best;
Reality would add to our unrest. . . .
We want no living Christ, whose truth intense
Pretends to no belief in our pretence
And, flashing on all folly and deceit,
Would blast our world to ashes at our feet. . . .
We do but ask to see
No more of Him below than is displayed
In the dead plaything our own hands have made
To lull our fears and comfort us in loss—
The wooden Christ upon a wooden Cross!

Who will dare to say that the poet's imagination has misled him? Men have always been ready, in sheer self-defence, to erect some vague idealistic image of Jesus in the temple of their spirits. But that is the image which we have to break, that the living Christ may reign.

"Reality would add to our unrest." Indeed it would. Hence the familiar hiatus between piety and practice, the scandal of the divorce between sacred and secular, between religion and the common life. Hence the intent debating of theological controversies totally irrelevant to human need. Hence the cult of a religion that is garrulous about minutiae of form and procedure, and dumb about social injustice: "straining at a gnat and swallowing a camel." Of all such obfuscations of the flaming challenge of Christ, John Oman once pungently declared: "A minister who can do it will go far; but the Church that does it is in its grave-clothes. People want to have everything in them spoken to except their consciences." Or in the blunt words of the late Bishop Gore, "We do like to lie to ourselves about ourselves!"

In every age the preaching of the Word has had to reckon with this perverse, tenacious mood. From the days of Amos and Isaiah to the present, "Prophesy unto us smooth things" has been an ever-recurring demand; and Gore, to quote him again, once averred that "the disease of modern preaching is its search after popularity." But it is the false prophet who plays down to men's craving for security when he ought to be showing them the lightnings of God flashing about their sins. "When God commands to take the trumpet," wrote John Milton in a famous passage, "and blow a dolorous or jarring blast, it lies not in man's will what he shall say, or what he shall conceal." The true prophets have never been pious dreamers and idealists, with their heads in the clouds. They have dealt with concrete situations and urgent realities: in the name of their God they have set up their banners against every wrecking force in the life of the world around them, and "Thus saith the Lord" has been their clarion cry.

The trouble is that there is something deep in human nature which objects to God, and will use even religion as a defence-mechanism against the thrust of reality. "The way to be successful," wrote Dr. W. R. Inge with a characteristically caustic touch, "is to give the

29

public exactly what it wants, and about ten per cent. more of it than it expects." "Don't go out for popularity," Spurgeon used to implore his students, "preach nothing down but the devil, and nothing up but Christ!"

It is quite impossible to preach Christ faithfully without saying many things which will sting the natural heart of man into opposition and rebellion. You will have to declare, for example, that to imagine one can receive God's forgiveness while refusing oneself to be forgiving to others is sophistry and deceit: a hard saying that for many. Or take the doctrine of the divine Fatherhood. There are still those who accept that doctrine and sun themselves in its warm and comforting glow, but resent being confronted with its disconcerting and inexorable implications in the realm of practical brotherhood and social ethics. "Give us the simple Gospel," they cry: escapism rationalizing itself again. Take even the missionary challenge and the conception of a universal Church. We believe that, just as no man is truly awake to-day who has not developed a supra-national horizon to his thinking, so no Church is anything more than a pathetic pietistic backwater unless it is first and fundamentally and all the time a world missionary Church. But there are stubborn strongholds into which that truth has yet to penetrate—minds which, for one reason or another, persistently regard the missionary enterprise as the province of a few enthusiasts, a side-show, an extra: not realizing that here is something which every professing Christian must espouse with all his heart and soul, or else surrender his right to march beneath the banners of Christ. It is your task as preachers to summon men to share with Jesus in the great crusade which began at Calvary and Pentecost, and shall never cease until the whole earth is filled with the glory of the Lord; and where the narrower view prevails, you must at all costs disturb its contentment and bid it reflect what it will feel like for any disciple to stand before Christ at last and say, "The world mission of Your religion had no help from me!"

Therefore resist all temptations to dilute your Gospel. Your task is not to send people away from church saying, "That was a lovely sermon" or "What an eloquent appeal!" The one question is: 'Did they, or did they not, meet God to-day? There will always be some who have no desire for that, some who rather than be confronted with the living Christ would actually prefer what G. K. Chesterton described as "one solid and polished cataract of platitudes flowing for ever and ever." But when St. Peter finished his first great sermon in Jerusalem, reported in the Book of Acts, I do not read that "when they heard this, they were intrigued by his eloquence," or "politely interested in his literary allusions," or "critical of his logic and his accent," or "bored and impassive and contemptuous"; what I do read is: "When they heard this, they were pierced to the heart." The heart of man has a whole armour of escapist devices to hold off the danger when reality comes too near. But I would remind you that Peter's theme that day—Jesus crucified and risen—is your basic message still: still as dynamic, as "mighty through God to the pulling down of strongholds," as moving and heart-piercing, as when men heard it preached in Jerusalem long ago.

There is, however, another side to the matter. Just as we noted how profoundly the modern mind is dominated by the tension between disillusionment and hope, so now we have to observe that over against the escapist attitude, countering it and setting up a further tension, there exists a strange passion for reality. Illogical? Undoubtedly. But there is the fact governing the relationship of multitudes at this moment to the religion of Christ—what repels, attracts; what disturbs and disconcerts, haunts and convinces. In the very moment of the headlong flight from reality, the drive towards reality makes itself felt; and "Depart from me, for I am a sinful man" becomes "Nearer, my God, to Thee!"

It is one of the mightiest safeguards of a man's ministry—to be aware of that hungry demand for reality breaking inarticulately from the hearts of those to whom he ministers. For that cry puts everything shoddy, second-hand or artificial utterly to shame.

You do not need to be eloquent, or clever, or sensational, or skilled in dialectic: you *must* be real. To fail there is to fail abysmally and tragically. It is to damage incalculably the cause you represent.

Anything savouring of unreality in the pulpit is a

double offence.   Let me urge upon you two considerations.

On the one hand, you will be preaching to people
who have been grappling all the week with stern
realities.   Behind a congregation assembling for worship there are stories of heavy anxiety and fierce
temptation, of loneliness and heroism, of overwork
and lack of work, of physical strain and mental wear
and tear.   We wrong them and we mock their struggles
if we preach our Gospel in abstraction from the hard
facts of their experience.   It is not only that they can
detect at once the hollowness of such a performance,
though that is true: there is also this—that to offer
pedantic theorizings and academic irrelevances to souls
wrestling in the dark is to sin against the Lord who
died for them and yearns for their redeeming.

But there is a further indictment of unreality in
preaching.   This is rooted not so much in the hard
problems men and women are facing—what Whittier
called this "maddening maze of things"—as in the
very nature of the Christian faith itself.   The Gospel
is quite shattering in its realism.   It shirks nothing.
It never seeks to gloss over the dark perplexities of
fate, frustration, sin and death, or to gild unpalatable
facts with a coating of pious verbiage or facile consolation.   It never side-tracks uncomfortable questions
with some naïve and cheerful cliché about providence
or progress.   It gazes open-eyed at the most menacing
and savage circumstance that life can show.   It is
utterly courageous.   Its strength is the complete

absence of utopian illusions. It thrusts Golgotha
upon men's vision and bids them look at that. The
very last charge which can be brought against the
Gospel is that of sentimentality, of blinking the facts.
It is devastating in its veracity, and its realism is a
consuming fire.

This is the message with which we are charged.
How grievous the fault if in our hands it becomes
tainted with unreality!

Of course, this is an issue which concerns the whole
Church, and not only the individual minister. Nothing
so gravely compromises the Christian witness as the
suspicion that organized religion is failing to practise
what it preaches. There are at least three directions
in which the Church to-day is having to meet and to
answer the challenge of the craving for reality. The
first relates to worship. Do our forms of worship
convey at every point the ringing note of entire sincerity and truth? The second has to do with the social
implications of the Gospel. Has it not happened all
too frequently that men of generous and noble nature,
tormented by the spectacle of the wrongs of society
and the sufferings of humanity, and on fire to help
their brethren "bound in affliction and iron," have
cried out against what seemed to them the appalling
torpor and inaction of the Church, dragging its slow
ponderous length along, with leisurely, lumbering
organization, and have flung away from it in impatience
and despair? The third challenge concerns Christian
unity. Is it legitimate, is it convincing, for a Church

to summon men to brotherhood and solidarity, while its own ruinous divisions are manifest to all? Is it real—in a day when the thrust and pressure of anti-Christian forces ought to be driving all believers to close their ranks and march together, in a day moreover when the reaction from the hyper-individualism of a bygone age is leading the younger generation to new experiments in the realm of community—is it real to maintain and perpetuate the partisan loyalties which disrupt true fellowship and drive Christians asunder? "Physician, heal thyself!"

In these ways, then, the demand for reality impinges upon the witness of the Church at large. But what mainly concerns us here is the more personal issue. If you are wise you will register a vow, at the very outset of your ministry, to make reality your constant quest. In the fine language of Scripture, "Her merchandise is better than silver, and the gain thereof than fine gold. She is more precious than rubies: and all the things thou canst desire are not to be compared unto her." Richard Baxter, who after three hundred years is still so sure a guide, has some plain-spoken words on this matter. "It is a lamentable case, that in a message from the God of heaven, of ever-lasting consequences to the souls of men, we should behave ourselves so weakly, so unhandsomely, so imprudently, or so slightly, that the whole business should miscarry in our hands, and God be dishonoured, and His work disgraced, and sinners rather hardened than converted." By way of contrast, take this signi-

ficant account of the effect produced by a great
nineteenth-century preacher on two of the most acute
and discriminating minds of his day. "We have just
been to hear Spurgeon," wrote Principal Tulloch,
describing a visit paid by Professor Ferrier the meta-
physician and himself to the Surrey Gardens Music
Hall one Sunday morning in 1858, "and have been
both so much impressed that I wish to give you my
impressions while they are fresh. As we came out we
both confessed, 'There is no doubt about *that*,' and I
was struck with Ferrier's remarkable expression, 'I
feel it would do me good to hear the like of that; it
sat so close to reality.' The sermon is about the most
real thing I have come in contact with for a long time."
That focuses the basic element of the true preacher's
power. "It sat so close to reality." *O si sic omnes!*

To make this quite concrete, let me urge upon you
the following maxims.

Be real in worship. If you are to lead others in
worship, you must be truly sharing in the act of worship
yourself. No doubt this sounds self-evident: yet it
does need to be emphasized. It means, for instance,
that you are not to occupy the time of hymn-singing
conning the Scripture lessons or fidgeting with a sheaf
of intimations or moving restlessly about the pulpit or
scanning the congregation for absentees. It is unnatural to bid your people lift up their hearts to the
Lord and then fail to join your voice with theirs in the
common act of praise. Moreover, it is by realizing
the attitude of worship in your own spirit that you will

best find deliverance from awkward mannerisms, from the blight of self-consciousness, and even from that deadly menace, the "pulpit voice," than which nothing is more infallibly destructive of the atmosphere of reality. And if you will remember that the sermon itself should be an act of worship, a sacramental showing forth of Christ, will not that save you from a multitude of pitfalls? You are not likely to become pompous or pretentious or pontifical if you are truly seeing Jesus and helping others to see Him. You will not scold or rate or lecture when God's Word is on your mouth. "Have you ever heard me preach?" Coleridge asked Charles Lamb one day; to which Lamb replied, "I never heard you do anything else." But it is a different preaching which creates the hush that tells when Christ is in the midst. There is nothing like worship, when it is real, for destroying every shred and atom of a man's self-importance. A minister of God who carries a sense of his importance about with him, even into the pulpit, is a dreadful and pathetic sight: but who will say it is unknown?

> There are a sort of men whose visages
> Do cream and mantle like a standing pond,
> And do a wilful stillness entertain,
> With purpose to be dress'd in an opinion
> Of wisdom, gravity, profound conceit;
> As who should say, "I am Sir Oracle,
> And when I ope my lips let no dog bark!"

Not that the corrective of a stiff and ostentatious for-

mality is to be a slovenly and casual informality!
"Some people imagine," declared the late Bernard
Manning of Cambridge, "that informality in the pulpit
in itself induces a belief in their sincerity or genius.
It induces only a belief in their bad taste, and makes us
want to get under the seats. Do not behave with a
triviality, a casualness, a haphazardness, as if not
merely God were absent, but as if all decent people
were absent too." There is one thing, and one thing
only, which can rescue the preacher from the immense
besetting dangers of his position, and that is to have
his own spirit bathed in the atmosphere of worship,
awed and subdued and thrilled that Christ should
come so near. In the words of a great tribute once
paid to John Brown of Haddington by no less a
critic than David Hume, "That's the man for me,
he means what he says: he speaks as if Jesus was at
his elbow."

Be real in language. Shun everything stilted,
grandiose, insipid or pedantic. Do not be like the
learned preacher who in the course of a sermon in a
village church remarked, "Perhaps some of you at
this point are suspecting me of Eutychianism." In your
business of bringing the Christian religion decisively
to bear upon the needs and problems of a twentieth-
century congregation, the language of Nicaea, or even
of the Westminster Divines, may be a hindrance rather
than a help. It is sheer slackness to fling at your
people great slabs of religious phraseology derived
from a bygone age, and leave them the task of re-

translation into terms of their own experience: that is your task, not theirs. Beware lest with facile platitudes and prosy commonplaces you cheapen the glorious Gospel of the blessed God. Eliminate everything which does not ring true. Be chary of indulging in oratory. "If a learned brother," said Spurgeon, "fires over the heads of his congregation with a grand oration, he may trace his elocution, if he likes, to Cicero and Demosthenes, but do not let him ascribe it to the Holy Spirit." If you have a tendency towards purple passages, suppress it sternly. A generation which is suspicious and impatient of high-sounding declamatory language in Parliament and press and on the public platform is not likely to be impressed by it in the pulpit; and if you once give men the idea that you are indulging in self-conscious artistry, they will hardly believe that the things of which you speak are overmastering realities. John Bunyan declares, in the Preface to *Grace Abounding*, "I could have stepped into a style much higher than this, and could have adorned all things more than here I have seemed to do." But he is quite candid about his reason for refusing such tricks of elegance and ornament: "I dare not. God did not play in tempting of me; neither did I play, when the pangs of hell caught hold upon me; wherefore I may not play in relating of them, but be plain and simple, and lay down the thing as it was." You are to be dealing in your preaching with real things: temptation, crushing grief, the fear of death, the grace of Christ. On such themes, you cannot indulge in florid writing and preciosity without seeming to deny their reality. "We talk now," exclaimed Joseph Parker, "about sermons being polished, and finished, and exquisite, with many a delicate little touch artistic. The Lord send fire upon all such abortions and burn them up, till their white ashes cannot any more be found!"

This is not to ban emotion from preaching. Any such advice would be supremely foolish. No man who realizes what is at stake—the depth of the human plight and the wonder of the divine remedy—will lack the authentic touch of passion. The preacher, said Lacordaire, is like Mount Horeb: "before God strikes him he is but a barren rock, but as soon as the divine hand has touched him, as it were with a finger, there burst forth streams that water the desert." What I would warn you against is not the genuine note of feeling that will carry your words like winged things into many a heart: it is that self-conscious straining after effect which may be legitimate in the schools of the sophists but is totally out of place at the mercy-seat of God. "Great sermons," declared Henry Ward Beecher, "are nuisances. Show-sermons are the temptation of the devil." Life and death issues are in your mouth when you preach the Gospel of Christ; and it is simply tragic trifling to make the sermon a declamatory firework show, or a garish display of the flowers of rhetoric. Have you ever marvelled at the Bible's sublime economy of words? Take a story like the coming of Ruth and Naomi. There is no striving after literary effect; the whole thing is told in short, quiet, almost staccato sentences; not a word is wasted. Yet how packed with emotion it is, how truly and profoundly moving! Or take the chapter which describes how David in the unguarded hour broke faith with his own soul and with God. Could any flamboyant eloquence of denunciation have equalled the overwhelming effect of those quiet words at the close: "But the thing that David had done displeased the Lord"? Above all, take the Passion narratives in the Gospels. How their restraint rebukes our vain embellishments! How crude and turgid those cherished purple passages begin to look in the light of the Word of God! Christ's messengers are sent forth armed with a Word able to break men's hearts and heal them. But remember—as Richard Baxter told the preachers of his day—"you cannot break men's hearts by patching up a gaudy oration." Be real in language!

Finally, I would say this: *Be real in your total attitude to the message.* There is something wrong if a man, charged with the greatest news in the world, can be listless and frigid and feckless and dull. Who is going to believe that the tidings brought by the preacher matter literally more than anything else on earth if they are presented with no sort of verve or fire or attack, and if the man himself is apathetic and uninspired, afflicted with spiritual coma, and unsaying by his attitude what he says in words? There is no prayer that ought to be more constantly on your lips than those lines of Charles Wesley, surely the most characteristic he ever wrote:

> O Thou who camest from above,
>   The pure celestial fire to impart,
> Kindle a flame of sacred love
>   On the mean altar of my heart.
> There let it for Thy glory burn.

Think of the news you are ordained to declare. That God has invaded history with power and great glory; that in the day of man's terrible need a second Adam has come forth to the fight and to the rescue; that in the Cross the supreme triumph of naked evil has been turned once for all to irrevocable defeat; that Christ is alive now and present through His Spirit; that through the risen Christ there has been let loose into the world a force which can transform life beyond recognition—this is the most momentous message human lips were ever charged to speak. It dwarfs all other truths into insignificance. It is electrifying in its power, shattering in its wonder. Surely it is desperately unreal to talk of themes like these in a voice deadened by routine, or in the maddeningly offhand and impassive manner which is all too familiar. It ought not to be possible to conduct a Church service in a way which leaves a stranger with the impression that nothing particular is happening and that no important business is on hand. "Went to Church to-day," wrote Robert Louis Stevenson in his journal, "and was not greatly depressed." If that is the best we can do for people, is it worth doing? "Certainly I must confess," cried Sir Philip Sidney, "I never heard the old song of Percy and Douglas, that I found not my heart moved more than with a trumpet." And to you has been committed the infinitely more heart-moving story of the Word made flesh: "that incredible interruption," wrote G. K. Chesterton, "as a blow that broke the very backbone of history." "It were better," he declared, "to rend our robes with a great cry against blasphemy, like Caiaphas in the judgment, rather than to stand stupidly debating fine shades of pantheism in the presence of so catastrophic a claim."

What strikes you about the preachers of the New Testament is that they had been swept off their feet and carried away by the glory of the great revelation. They went to men who had sinned disastrously, and they cried, "Listen! We can tell you of reconciliation and a new beginning." They went to others who had nothing but the vaguest fatalism for a religion, and they proclaimed exultingly the love of the eternal Father. They went to desolate and weak and lonely souls, and with shouts of confidence exclaimed, "Lift up your heads! You can do all things through Christ who strengthens you." They went to others shivering in cold terror at the thought of death's onward inexorable march, and they bade them "Rejoice! Christ has conquered. Death lies dead!" It is the same tremendous tidings for which the world is hungry yet. To discover, after a hundred defeats, that it is still possible in Christ to make a fresh beginning; to have distrusted God for half a lifetime of prayerless years, and then to be told that He cares intensely, and that the way to His heart lies open now; to have felt utterly inadequate for life's demands and for the wear and tear of worrying days, and then to learn of vast incalculable reserves of power just waiting to be used; to have had nothing to look forward to but the snapping of the ties that matter most, and then to find that death has ceased to count, because victory and immortality belong to love—this is the glorious news, too often, alas, made dull and commonplace by our poor bungling, and desupernaturalised by our stolidity and ineptitude.

Suppose the apostles were to come back to earth to-day, and watch us at our weekly worship. Would they recognize the religion in whose dawn they had found it such bliss to be alive? Might they not have to say, "What has happened? Is this the faith that once stirred the world like a thousand trumpets? Is this the miraculous religion that burnt us with its flame? How can these our descendants repeat with the chill of lackadaisical boredom words that once awakened the dead? 'God was incarnate': can they say that, and not be thrilled and dazzled by the amazement of it? 'The Son of God was crucified, dead, and buried': can they think of that and not be overwhelmed by its awful meaning? 'Christ is risen': can they tell that, and not want to shout for the glory of it? Why have they allowed these breathlessly exciting facts to be written in the dull catalogue of common things and

suffocated by the formalities of a routine religion?
Why seek ye the living among the dead?''

"Were there but such clear and deep impressions
upon our souls," wrote Richard Baxter, "of the
glorious things that we daily preach, O what a change
it would make in our sermons and in our private
course. I marvel how I can preach of them slightly
and coldly. I seldom come out of the pulpit but my
conscience smiteth me that I have been no more
serious and fervent. 'How could'st thou speak of life
and death with such a heart?'" The fact is that all
our assiduous planning for increased efficiency in
organized religion will lead to nothing unless we have
a Church which is tingling and vibrating with the
wonder of its own evangel. Then, only then, will the
Christian forces make their God-intended impact on
the world; and then we shall begin to understand the
saying that is written: "The zeal of Thy house hath
eaten me up."

I am not suggesting that you should simulate a
warmth and passion which you do not feel. Such
"synthetic unction," as Dr. W. R. Maltby has called
it, "may impress simple souls, but it corrupts the
preacher. Emotion arises out of the truth: emotion-
alism is poured on to it." That is the great difference.
But you will need no cheap substitute for the real
thing if you are living close to Christ. Your heart will
burn within you as He talks with you by the way; and
something of that inner glow will communicate itself
to your preaching, and kindle a flame in other lives.

This will be true, not only of sermons belonging to what is sometimes called the prophetic function of the ministry, but also of those in which the teaching note predominates. A ministry extending over many years in one place can be effective and fruitful only if much of its strength is given to systematic exposition of the Bible and regularly planned instruction on the great doctrines of the Christian faith. But what I am concerned to insist on at the moment is that even your teaching sermons ought to have in them, and can have, something of the authentic thrill of the evangel. Do not believe the defeatist moan that the production of two vital sermons each week is neither mentally nor spiritually possible. For if there are indeed "unsearchable riches" in Christ, you will always be pioneering and exploring, always discovering new depths in the Gospel, and the streams of the river of life will never for you run dry. The longest ministry is too short by far to exhaust the treasures of the Word of God. Certainly if you preach your own theories and ideas, using Scripture texts merely as pegs to hang them on, you will soon be at the end of your resources —and the sooner the better. But if you will let the Scriptures speak their own message, if you will realize that every passage or text has its own quite distinctive meaning, you will begin to feel that the problem is not lack of fresh material, but the very embarrassment of riches; and with the Psalmist you will cry, "I rejoice at Thy Word, as one that findeth great spoil." Thus in teaching and exposition no less than in direct

evangelism, in your continual task of instructing your
people in the whole counsel of God no less than in the
act of appealing for decision, the message will be alive,
throbbing with vital force, imbued with the redeeming
energy of the Holy Spirit: "quick and powerful, and
sharper than any two-edged sword." No one will
doubt or question its reality.

It was this characteristic which R. W. Dale of
Birmingham noted in the work of D. L. Moody. "He
preached in a manner which produced the sort of effect
produced by Luther. He exulted in the free grace of
God. His joy was contagious. Men leaped out of
darkness into light, and lived a Christian life afterwards." There is no reason why your ministry, in its
own degree, should not achieve visible results, provided
you keep alive within you a sense of the wonder of the
facts you preach and of the urgency of the issues with
which you deal. Every Sunday morning when it comes
ought to find you awed and thrilled by the reflection—
"God is to be in action to-day, through me, for these
people: this day may be crucial, this service decisive,
for someone now ripe for the vision of Jesus." Remember that every soul before you has its own story
of need, and that if the Gospel of Christ does not meet
such need nothing on earth can. Aim at results.
Expect mighty works to happen. Realize that, al-
though your congregation may be small, every soul is
infinitely precious. Never forget that Christ Himself,
according to His promise, is in the midst, making the
plainest and most ordinary church building into the

house of God and the gate of heaven. Hear His voice saying, "This day is the Scripture fulfilled in your ears. This day is salvation come to this house." Then preaching, which might otherwise be a dead formality and a barren routine, an implicit denial of its own high claim, will become a power and a passion; and the note of strong, decisive reality, like a trumpet, will awaken the souls of men.

III

Up to this point, we have been considering the preacher's task as influenced by two crucial factors in the contemporary scene: the tension between disillusionment and hope, and the tension between escapism and realism. We turn now finally to a third characteristic mood with which we have to reckon in our presentation of the Gospel to this age. This is the critical tension between *Scepticism and Faith.* You are going out to a world which is literally "in a strait betwixt two," torn by an inner conflict between the spirit of denial and the spirit of affirmation, between the loud self-confident dogmatism of the thoroughgoing sceptic and the deep wistfulness of the seeker after God. "Poore intricated soule!" cried John Donne long ago, contemplating the unresolved tensions of man's nature, "Riddling, perplexed, labyrinthicall soule!"

That there has been, on the one hand, a widespread failure of belief is all too apparent. Evidences of it

48

can be found in the neglect of public worship; in the indifference to the Bible; in the astounding ignorance even amongst well-educated people as to what Christianity really is; and in the prevalence of the type of humanism we have already referred to, which dethrones God and sets man in the centre of the picture. The causes of the sceptical mood are various. Some have been driven from the citadel of faith by the formidable assaults of science. Others have found their religious beliefs crumbling away before the ruthless, terrifying aspect of a world at war. Others have felt the desolating stab of doubt and misgiving as they grappled with the mystery of suffering. Many have lost the vision through failure to maintain a disciplined devotional life. Many have lacked the necessary powers of resistance to ward off the infection of a predominantly secularist society.

There, then, is the challenge you are called upon to meet. I am not thinking now of that flippant, superficial type of scepticism which will stand in the presence of the profoundest mysteries without a trace of awe or wonder, which will talk jauntily of its emancipation from the ethics of Christ, and smile patronizingly at the prayers of the saints, and look with pity upon those who still frequent the worship and ordinances of the Church. Nor am I thinking of the intellectually half-baked scepticism which has a naturalistic explanation for every phenomenon of the religious life, which calls prayer auto-suggestion, and conscience a utilitarian social contract, and immortality flagrant wishful-thinking, and God a projection of the human mind: as if such a travesty of the facts, such a "weary, stale, flat, and unprofitable" jargon, compounded of bad psychology and unintelligent rationalism, could cancel out the witness of the Christian centuries, or be the dynamite to blast and to destroy the Rock of ages! I am thinking rather of the deeper and more serious challenge which accosts our ministry in this age when beliefs which once seemed inviolable are fighting for their very life, and when the faith of multitudes of our fellow-men has gone down defeated before the wild surge and onset of militant doubt. Have you, as Christ's ambassadors, the word of the Lord for such a situation? Can you confront it with the decisive testimony of an irrefragable first-hand experience? "I believe," cried the psalmist, "therefore have I spoken." It is a great thing to be able, like the apostle, to add: "We also believe, and therefore speak."

To be aware, however, of the prevalent mood of scepticism and of the widespread failure of belief is not enough. For beneath the surface there is an acute tension: the thesis and antithesis of doubt and faith, the drive of the spirit of denial, and the urge of the quest for God. Do not allow the drift away from the Church, and the apparent indifference and even hostility to organized religion, to deceive you. Everywhere to-day, even in the least likely places, there are men dimly seeking the Lord, "if haply they might feel after

Him, and find Him." You will remember how the
invincible wistfulness of faith kept glimmering even
through the scepticism of Thomas Hardy:

> That with this bright believing band
> I have no claim to be,
> That faiths by which my comrades stand
> Seem fantasies to me,
> And mirage-mist their Shining Land,
> Is a strange destiny.

Surely if we had ears to hear and eyes to see, we should
recognize the same deep ache and yearning to-day even
in lives apparently devoid of Christian convictions,
lacking any conscious background of God for their
thinking and activity, with no flame of prayer on the
altar of their spirits, and no conception of a risen,
regnant Christ who has overcome the sharpness of
death and opened the Kingdom of Heaven to all
believers. To all intents and purposes, the sceptical
mood and the assault of doubt and denial have choked
their spiritual life, as the Philistines choked the wells
of Abraham in the valley of Gerar long ago; but you
will find, as Isaac did, that the underground wells are
still there, buried but undestroyed, and needing only
the touch of faith and love to set them flowing free
again. That is the measure of your opportunity.

Signs are indeed not wanting that the sceptical mood
is less sure of itself to-day than a generation ago. Its
armour has been pierced. Its self-confidence has been
badly shaken. You will not be handicapped, as were

some of your predecessors, by having to preach a spiritual view of the world to an age drugged with the narcotic of a thoroughgoing materialism. "We are no longer tempted," wrote Eddington in *Science and the Unseen World*, "to condemn the spiritual aspects of our nature as illusory because of their lack of concreteness. We have travelled far from the standpoint which identifies the real with the concrete." Many who in the heyday of revolt and emancipation threw over the trammels of orthodoxy are beginning to suspect that the Christian interpretation of life may after all be more credible, more intellectually respectable, than any of the alternatives. Robert Browning's dramatic defence of the faith in *Bishop Blougram* is doubly cogent now. What the poet saw with piercing clearness was that, if the difficulties facing belief are bad enough, those confronting unbelief are much worse; and that all that scepticism does is to land the mind in problems far more intractable and embarrassing than those it is seeking to escape. This is the fact which is forcing itself into recognition again at the present hour. Hence you start your ministry with an immense advantage. Multitudes of people to-day are haunted by the suspicion that the world is perfectly meaningless apart from God. That is a good atmosphere in which to have to preach the Gospel. If you can bring to troubled hearts the assurance that the Christian faith does make sense of the universe and give a credible interpretation of life, if you can show them God at the heart of their experience, you need never fear that your word will return unto you void, nor that your ministry will be suggestive of the sounding brass and the tinkling cymbal. The sceptical mood has had its innings, and has failed to satisfy. Therefore "lift up thy voice with strength; lift it up, be not afraid; say unto the cities of Judah, Behold your God!"

You will do well to remember that, whenever you speak to men in the name of Jesus Christ, unseen instincts deep within them are reinforcing your words.

> Thou hast great allies;
> Thy friends are exultations, agonies,
> And love, and man's unconquerable mind.

"The belief in God," said Rabbi Duncan, "presses multifariously upon man." Let that be your confidence!

You do not preach in a vacuum. Those secret allies of God are always there, working in the hearts of those to whom you are sent. One of the greatest is the sense of sin. However much men may romanticize the guilty conscience, or rationalize with clever casuistry the restless misery of the disintegrated and dishevelled soul, there are stubborn questions which refuse to be silenced: How shall I make my peace with God? Can the damage be atoned for? Can the frightful dilemma be resolved?

> O how shall I, whose native sphere
>   Is dark, whose mind is dim,
> Before the Ineffable appear,
> And on my naked spirit bear
>   The uncreated beam?

53

Another of those secret allies on which you can count in your ministry is the human heart's need of comfort. Was it not Ian Maclaren who, near the end, declared that if he could begin his life-work over again he would strike the note of comfort far oftener than he had done? The amount of trouble in the average congregation is far greater than any unimaginative onlooker would ever guess. So many who face the world gallantly and uncomplainingly are wearing hidden sackcloth next their hearts: "men of sorrows, and acquainted with grief." "Who but my selfe," cried John Donne in a sermon in London in 1626, "can conceive the sweetnesse of that salutation when the Spirit of God sayes to me in a morning, Go forth to-day and preach, and preach consolation, preach peace, preach mercy?" And when the Spirit of God thrusts you forth on that same compassionate errand, your words—if you are careful to avoid all sentimentality, and to offer only the strong, bracing comfort of the New Testament, the authentic *paraklesis*— will make a highroad to many hearts.

But best of all God's secret allies in the souls to whom you preach is the eternity God Himself has planted there, the hunger for the bread of heaven. Often only an inarticulate craving, concealed deliberately sometimes behind a mask of apathy and irreligion, it is nevertheless the decisive element in the situation and the supremely hopeful factor of your ministry. No man's soul can be satisfied indefinitely with the wretched husks of a materialist philosophy. It begins to starve for something better than such poor earthly stuff. Sooner or later, the famine grips it. It grows homesick. Try as it may, it can never quite delude itself into believing that the atmosphere of a secular society is its native air. It wants to fling its windows open towards Jerusalem. It cries aloud for the God who is its home. The blank space in the modern heart, said Julian Huxley, is a "God-shaped blank." How can preaching ever die out while these things are so? Do not listen to the foolish talk which suggests that, for this twentieth century, the preaching of the Word is an anachronism, and that the pulpit, having served its purpose, must now be displaced by press or radio, discussion group or Brains Trust, and finally vanish from the scene. As long as God sets His image on the soul, and men are restless till they rest in Him, so long will the preacher's task persist, and his voice be heard through all the clamour of the world.

It ought to fill you with something of the glad fearlessness of the apostolic preachers, the *parresia* of the New Testament, to know that, even before you open your mouth to speak, God's secret allies have been at work in the hearts of those now waiting for the Word. It will save you from the false diffidence of misplaced apologetic. Shame on our apologizing for the truth of Christ! Shame on our timid offering of some pithless Gospel denuded of the supernatural, dull unkindled ethics with a Christian tinge, views and impressions of current events with a smattering of the Sermon on the Mount, tame humanistic exhortations to brotherhood and neighbourliness and the observance of the Golden Rule! Cannot we hear the hearts of men crying for the living God? Do we think Christ purchased the Church with His blood that it should be only a depository of doctrine, only a social conscience, only a glorified discussion group? Nothing about a Church—no culture or enlightenment, no assiduous attention to the details of organization, no elaborate machinery of good works—can avail anything or compensate one atom for the radical defect, if it is not a place where men and women can come quite sure that their hungry hearts will find the living bread.

Have you that gift to offer? In the last resort, everything depends on the inner certainty of your own soul. Two hundred years ago, George Whitefield preached a sermon in Glasgow on *The Duty of a Gospel Minister*. "You will never preach," he said, "with power feelingly, while you deal in a false commerce with truths unfelt. It will be but poor, dry, sapless stuff—your people will go away out of the church as cold as they came in. For my own part," he cried, "I would not preach an unknown Christ for ten thousand worlds. Such offer God strange fire, and their sermons will but increase their own damnation." Izaak Walton has described John Donne in the pulpit of St. Paul's, "preaching the Word so, as shewed his own heart was possest with those very thoughts and joyes that he labored to distill into others." Does not that lay bare our deepest need? We want something better than second-hand religion and borrowed theology, and stolid unkindled Churches which are merely efficient and competent machines, dealing with reality at a distance and sending earnest seekers away with an aching, disappointed sense that something vital is lacking. We want that thrilling sense of immediacy, that directness of touch, that spiritual drive and momentum, which only a personal encounter with God can ever impart. "It is good," declared Phillips Brooks, "to be a Herschel who describes the sun; but it is better to be a Prometheus who brings the sun's fire to the earth." "I came into the town," wrote John Wesley in his *Journal*, "and offered them Christ." To spend your days doing that—not just describing Christianity or arguing for a creed, not apologizing for the faith or debating fine shades of religious meaning, but actually offering and giving men Christ—could any life-work be more thrilling or momentous?

Chapter II

THE PREACHER'S THEME

" From the beginning of time until now, this is the only thing that has ever really happened. When you understand this you will understand all prophecies, and all history."
Dorothy L. Sayers, *The Man Born to be King*.

IN that profoundly moving book, Tolstoy's *War and Peace*, one of the most memorable scenes describes the night at Russian Headquarters when a messenger brought to Koutouzow, the old Commander-in-Chief, the first news of Napoleon's retreat from Moscow. After the years of terrific strain and agony to which the soul of Russia had been subjected, the tidings sounded incredible. The envoy finished his report and then waited for orders in silence. A Staff Officer was about to speak, but Koutouzow checked him with his hand, and tried to say something himself. Not a word would come. Finally the old man turned away to where the sacred images stood against the wall. And then suddenly and unrestrainedly, "Great God," he cried, "my Lord and Creator! Thou hast heard my prayer! Russia is saved!" And then he burst into tears.

To-day the envoy of the Gospel is charged with tidings more moving and more wonderful by far. If this message is fantasy, there is no hope for humanity anywhere. If this is true, the whole world is saved.

We proceed, therefore, to a consideration of the

content of the message. What is the preacher's theme?

Some years ago there appeared a composite volume with the intriguing title *If I Had Only One Sermon to Preach*. It was an interesting experiment: yet one suspects that upon most of the contributors the necessity of including the whole of revelation within the narrow limits of one all-comprehensive sermon must have exercised a somewhat depressing influence and imposed a considerable handicap. It would prove too much even for an apostle. You will find that your best sermons—best in the sense of being most truly charged with spiritual power—are not those you compose when the mood seizes you to write something outstanding and exceptional and definitive; in all probability, not even those you construct with special occasions in view; on the contrary, your best sermons will get themselves made in the ordinary course of your ministry week by week. You are likely in the good providence of God to have not only one sermon to preach but hundreds, and you must order your methods accordingly: so that over a course of months and years your sermons will balance and correct one another in their emphasis on different aspects of what the apostle called the "many-coloured" wisdom of God. You will soon discover that one of the most important arts you have to learn is the art of omission. You have apostolic authority for endeavouring to "become all things to all men"; but Paul never suggested that the right way to do it was to pack a little of everything into every sermon, mixing your ingredients in order to have something in the dish for every palate! There is a cautionary recipe in an eighteenth-century book for the making of a salad. It specifies scores of different delicacies, and bids the ingenuous cook add a little of this, a touch of that, a flavour of something else, until every imaginable ingredient has been included; then somewhat sardonically it goes on to say, "After mixing well, open a large window and throw out the whole mess." To concentrate too much into one miscellaneous masterpiece—whether it be a salad or a sermon—is the surest way to fail. All sermons should indeed be crammed with the Gospel, and it is nothing less than "the whole counsel of God" that you are commissioned to declare; but to say that all sermons should comprise every facet of Christian doctrine is absurd. "There are those highly illuminated beings," complained Joseph Parker, "who expect a whole scheme of theology in every discourse. I trust," he added, "they will be starved to death."

There is, however, another sense in which the thought behind the title *If I Had Only One Sermon to Preach* may prove salutary; and Richard Baxter's injunction—"preach as a dying man to dying men" —is not simply to be discounted as morbid hyperbole. For every gathering of God's people for worship is a quite distinctive event; and though a congregation may meet twice a Sunday all the year round, no such event ever exactly repeats itself. Always there are differentiating circumstances; always "Now is the accepted time." One thing at least is clear: we have no right in our preaching to waste time on side-issues and irrelevances. In other words, if we are not determined that in every sermon Christ is to be preached, it were better that we should resign our commission forthwith and seek some other vocation. Alexander Whyte, describing his Saturday walks and talks with Marcus Dods, declared: "Whatever we started off with in our conversations, we soon made across country, somehow, to Jesus of Nazareth, to His death, and His resurrection, and His indwelling"; and unless our sermons make for the same goal, and arrive at the same mark, they are simply beating the air. It was a favourite dictum of the preachers of a bygone day that, just as from every village in Britain there was a road which, linking on to other roads, would bring you to London at last, so from every text in the Bible, even the remotest and least likely, there was a road to Christ. Possibly there were occasions when strange turns of exegesis and dubious allegorizings were pressed into service for the making of that road; but the instinct was entirely sound which declared that no preaching which failed to exalt Christ was worthy to be called Christian preaching. This is our great master-theme. In the expressive, forthright language of John Donne: "All knowledge that begins not, and ends not with His glory, is but a giddy, but a vertiginous circle, but an elaborate and exquisite ignorance."

I

But what does it mean—to "preach Christ"? The phrase calls for definition. I suggest that you should go, for the true touchstone in this matter, to the preaching of the early Church. When Henry Ward Beecher began his ministry, he was baffled by a disappointing absence of results and an almost total lack of response. The chariot wheels dragged; there were no signs of an awakening; the indifferent remained sunk in their indifference. But one day the thought gripped him: "There was a reason why, when the apostles preached, they succeeded, and I will find it out if it is to be found out." That was sound strategy, and it had an immediate reward. It would be well for us if a similar experience should drive us back to the New Testament, to search for the secret of the first generation of preachers of the Word. What was this message which consumed these men like a flame, and through them kindled the world?

It is worth noticing, to begin with, what it was not. It was not a theory or an idea. It was not something they had arrived at by the processes of their own thought and research. It was neither an argument with paganism, nor a panegyric on brotherhood; neither ethical exhortation, nor religious edification; neither mystical experience, nor spiritual uplift. It was not even a reproduction of the Sermon on the Mount; nor was it an account of their subjective reaction to the teaching and example of their Lord.

In its essence, it was none of these things. Doubtless it included some of them, but basically it was quite
different. It was the announcement of certain concrete facts of history, the heralding of real, objective
events. Its keynote was, "That which we have seen
and heard declare we unto you." Declaration, not
debate, was its characteristic attitude. The driving-
force of the early Christian mission was not
propaganda of beautiful ideals of the brotherhood
of man; it was proclamation of the mighty acts
of God.

What were these historic events thus heralded far
and wide? There were two events, which in reality
were not two but one. "Christ died for our sins."
That was fundamental. At the very heart of the
apostles' message stood the divine redemptive deed on
Calvary. But this literally crucial event was never in
their preaching isolated from the other which crowned
and completed it, forming as it were the keystone of
the arch. In the terse language of the Book of Acts,
they preached "Jesus and the Resurrection." "So we
preach," wrote Paul summarily to the Corinthians,
"and so ye believed." It is worth remembering that
when towards the end he was indicted before Festus
and Agrippa, it was this unceasing witness to the
Resurrection which formed the major count in the
charge his accusers brought against him. All the
trouble centred in "one Jesus, which was dead, whom
Paul affirmed to be alive." In other words, the
Resurrection—so far from being dragged in or tacked

on to the Gospel of the Cross—was implicit in every word the preachers spoke.

But they went further. For they declared that in these two shattering events, now seen to be one, the Kingdom of God had broken in with power. Its consummation still lay out of sight, waiting for the fulness of the time and the completion of the purposes of God; but the new epoch foretold by the prophets had actually dawned. From the realm of the invisible beyond, the one far-off divine event had suddenly projected itself into history. What had formerly been pure eschatology was there before their eyes: the supernatural made visible, the Word made flesh. No longer were they dreaming of the Kingdom age: they were living in it. It had arrived. This was the essential crisis of the hour.

They went still further. The death and the resurrection of Jesus, they said, were nothing less than God in omnipotent action. What assailed the crowds in the streets of Jerusalem at Pentecost was no abstract scheme of salvation; nor was it the story of a spiritual genius who had gone about continually doing good, uttering beautiful thoughts about the divine Fatherhood and the whole duty of man, and founding a new religion. It was the stupendous tidings, dwarfing all other facts whatever, that the sovereign Power of the universe had cleft history asunder, travelling in the greatness of His strength, mighty to save. "We do hear them speak in our tongues," they cried, "the wonderful works of God." This was the apostolic theme. This was the characteristic *kerygma* of the Church. And its power was irresistible.

I have dwelt on this, because it bears so directly on the contemporary situation and on our own work as preachers. There is an extraordinary amount of vagueness, even among enlightened people, as to what Christianity really is. One recalls a striking passage in Galsworthy where Jolyon and his son are discussing things together and the talk turns to religion. "'Do you believe in God, Dad? I've never known.' 'What do you mean by God?' he said; 'there are two irreconcilable ideas of God. There's the Unknowable Creative Principle—one believes in That. And there's the Sum of altruism in man—naturally one believes in That.' 'I see. That leaves out Christ, doesn't it?' Jolyon stared. Christ, the link between those two ideas! Out of the mouths of babes!'" But you will find to-day that, even where Christ is brought in, the vagueness is apt to persist; and in many quarters there are only the haziest notions of what it means to be a Christian. The Gospel is regarded as a codification of human ideals and aspirations; religious instruction means teaching the ethic of the Sermon on the Mount; Jesus is the noblest pattern of the good life. This, it is assumed, is basic Christianity: anything which goes beyond it is "sectarian theology," mere debatable theory. What this view fails utterly to realize is that the Christian religion is not primarily a discussion of desirable human virtues and qualities—not that at all —but a message about God: not a summary of the ways men ought to act in an ideal society, but an account of the way in which God has acted in history decisively and for ever.

There can be no doubt that for this prevalent vagueness the Church itself must accept some share of the blame. Too often we have wandered away from our true centre. Perhaps almost unconsciously we have shifted the emphasis from where the apostles put it. We have become entangled in side-issues. We have concentrated too little on the primal verities of the faith, too much on what Phillips Brooks once called "the bric-à-brac of theology." Do not misunderstand me. I am not arguing against detailed instruction in the implications of our holy religion for life and character and conduct. On the contrary, I believe that an interpretation of the Gospel in terms of its ethical, social and economic challenge is to-day an urgent necessity. Dr. L. P. Jacks was entirely right to remind us that "every truth that religion announces passes insensibly into a command. Its indicatives are veiled imperatives." But what I am concerned to assert is that in the Christian religion the indicatives are basic and fundamental. And nothing could be more marrowless and stultified and futile than the preaching which is for ever exhorting "Thus and thus you must act," and neglecting the one thing which essentially makes Christianity: "Thus has God acted, once and for all."

> Glorious—more glorious, is the crown
> Of Him that brought salvation down,
> By meekness called thy Son:

Thou that stupendous truth believed;
And now the matchless deed's achieved,
DETERMINED, DARED, and DONE.

Surely it is a great thing to realize that, just as the
early Church knew itself commissioned for something
far more vital and incisive than vague talk about topical
problems, far more dynamic and explosive than the
propagating of interesting ideas or the fostering of a
new type of piety, so you are being sent forth to-day to
thrust God upon men, to announce that in the fact of
Christ God has bridged the gulf between two worlds,
has shattered the massive tyranny of the powers of
darkness, has changed radically and for ever the human
prospect and the total aspect of the world, and brought
life and immortality to light! Here is no academic
speculation or cold, insipid moralizing; here is no dull
collection of views and impressions, schemes and
theories; here is a Gospel, able to bind up the broken-
hearted, proclaim deliverance to the captives, and bid
a distracted world stand still and see the glory of the
coming of the Lord.

How foolish, then, the clamour for non-doctrinal
preaching! And how desperately you will impoverish
your ministry if you yield to that demand! The under-
lying assumption is, of course, that doctrine is dull: a
perfectly absurd misapprehension. It is indeed lamentably true that the sublimest doctrine can be treated in
a way that will reduce the average congregation to
leaden apathy and boredom. "Buy a theological
barrel-organ, brethren," growled Spurgeon scathingly,

"with five tunes accurately adjusted!" John Keats complained that "Philosophy will clip an angel's wings, unweave a rainbow"; and he might have added that there is a formal type of preaching which all too successfully clips the wings of wonder and unweaves the rainbow arch of the salvation of God. But to maintain that doctrine, as such, is necessarily a dull affair is simply a confession of ignorance or downright spiritual deficiency. Only a crass blindness could fail to see that such a truth as that presented in the sentence "The Word was made flesh" is overpoweringly dramatic in itself and utterly revolutionary in its consequences. "If this is dull," exclaims Dorothy Sayers, "then what, in Heaven's name, is worthy to be called exciting?"

This, I believe, is the true answer to the anxiety which haunts many a young minister at the outset of his work, the anxiety lest he may exhaust the subject-matter of the faith he has to preach long before his course is run. Take comfort! Enshrined at the heart of the faith are facts of such perennial vitality and incalculable force that you will never, to your dying day, tell more than a fraction of the truth that God has blazed across your sky. "We preach always Him," declared Luther, "the true God and man. This may seem a limited and monotonous subject, likely to be soon exhausted, but we are never at the end of it." Why should you imagine that the stimulating atmosphere of expectation which surrounds you at the opening of your ministry must inevitably give way sooner or later to a sultry air of tedious disenchantment? Does spring, regularly returning year by year, ever become monotonous? Is not its wonder as fresh and unspoilt still as when the morning stars sang together and the sons of God shouted for joy? And are God's mighty acts in history and redemption less enthralling than His mighty acts in nature? Drop dogma from your preaching, and for a brief time you may titillate the fancy of the superficial, and have them talking about your cleverness; but that type of ministry wears out speedily, and garners no spiritual harvest in the end. Therefore settle it with your own souls now that, whatever else you may do or leave undone, you will preach in season and out of season God's redemptive deed in Christ. This is the one inexhaustible theme. "We may call that doctrine exhilarating," writes Dorothy Sayers again, "or we may call it devastating; we may call it revelation or we may call it rubbish; but if we call it dull, then words have no meaning at all." I am not counselling you to keep harping on one string, for variety is the very breath of life in preaching. I am insisting on what is paradoxical but true—that the more resolutely and stubbornly you refuse to be deflected from the one decisive theme, the greater the variety you will achieve; while the more you seek variety by wandering from your centre, the faster the descent to bathos and monotony. God's deed in Christ touches life at every point. It speaks to every aspect of the human predicament. It stretches all horizons illimitably. It bursts through

the narrow orbit of habitual thought-forms, hackneyed
social attitudes, doctrinal predilections. There is no
plummet that can sound this ocean's depth, no yard-
stick that can measure the length and breadth of this
Jerusalem. And the surest way to keep your ministry
living and vigorous and immune from the blight of
spiritual lassitude and drudgery is to draw continually
upon the unsearchable riches which in Christian doctrine are lying to your hand; and to remember that
you—no less than the New Testament preachers—are
commissioned for the purpose of *kerygma*, the proclamation of news, the heralding of the wonderful
works of God.

II

Now here we come in sight of that much-debated
question: What is the relationship between preaching
and worship? You are doubtless aware that there
exists to-day a tendency to set preaching and worship
in opposition. According to this view, the prayers
and praises of the sanctuary, and the celebration of the
Sacraments, are divine, in the sense that there we have
direct touch with God; whereas preaching is merely
human, as representing reflections, appeals and exhortations issuing from the mind of man. It is
characteristic of this attitude to disparage preaching,
to regret that the sermon should ever have come to
hold so important a place in the services of the House
of Prayer, and even to hint that the position it occupies
is a subtle form of selfishness, detracting from the

glory of God. No doubt this view is largely to be explained as a reaction from the disgraceful custom of regarding prayers and praises as mere "preliminaries" to something more important to follow: a horrid caricature of true worship, which to-day would be almost universally repudiated. But surely it is deplorable that some, going to the opposite extreme, should deny to preaching any integral place in the context of the act of worship, or at best should tolerate it as an intrusion, regrettable but inevitable, of the human element into what is essentially divine. The ominous thing about such an attitude is the complete misunderstanding it betrays, not only of the preacher's function, but even of the nature of the Christian faith. If Christianity were the formulation of a body of human ideals; if the pulpit were a public platform for the dissemination of personal opinions or the propagation of a party programme; if the preacher were a kind of religious commentator on current events; if his main function were to explore the contemporary situation and to diagnose the malady of society; if the sermon were a literary lecture, a medicinal dose of psychological uplift, or a vehicle for the giving of good advice—the distinction between preaching and worship would be justified. But, in fact, that distinction is based either on a seriously defective understanding of the Gospel itself, or on a refusal to realize what happens when the Gospel is truly preached. If Christianity is indeed the revelation of God, and not the research of man; if preaching is the proclamation of a message which has come not merely through human lips, but out from the deeps of the eternal ; if the preacher is sent (in St. Paul's expressive phrase) to "placard" Christ, to declare a Word which is not his own, because it is the Word of God Incarnate—it follows that the attempt to segregate preaching from worship is fundamentally false. The fact is that the sermon is divinely intended to be one of those high places of the spirit where men and women grow piercingly aware of the eternal, and where a worshipping congregation—forgetting all about the preacher—sees "no man, save Jesus only." And ours must have been a singularly barren and unfortunate experience if we have never, when sitting in church listening to the preaching of the Word, been moved to adoration, never seen the angels ascending and descending on the ladder linking Bethel to the world unseen, and never whispered to ourselves, "This is none other but the house of God, this is the gate of heaven."

In this connection, I would recall to your minds the famous passage in Robert Wodrow's *Analecta*, where an English merchant of three hundred years ago describes to his friends in London certain preachers he had heard during a business visit to Scotland. At St. Andrews he had listened to Robert Blair. "That man," he said, "showed me the majesty of God." Afterwards he had heard "a little fair man" preach— this was Samuel Rutherford: "and that man showed me the loveliness of Christ." Then at Irvine he had heard a discourse by "a well-favoured, proper old man"—David Dickson: "and that man showed me all my heart." These, surely, are the supreme functions of preaching in every age. And if these things are happening, if in a congregation one soul here and another there may be receiving, as the sermon proceeds, some vision of the majesty of God, some glimpse of the loveliness of Christ, some revelation of personal need beneath the searchlight of the Spirit, is the ministry of the Word to be minimized, or regarded as less divine, more doubtfully devotional, than other parts of the service? Is not such preaching worship?

The late Archbishop of Canterbury, Dr. William Temple, once propounded a thesis which, he admitted, many people would feel to be outrageous and fantastic. "This world," he said, "can be saved from political chaos and collapse by one thing only, and that is worship." Certainly, as it stands, that dictum may look eccentric and absurd. But Dr. Temple proceeded to define what worship is. (Notice how significantly the three elements enshrined in Wodrow's story make here their reappearance.) "To worship is to quicken the conscience by the holiness of God, to feed the mind with the truth of God, to purge the imagination by the beauty of God, to open the heart to the love of God, to devote the will to the purpose of God." But are not these precisely the aims and ends of all genuine preaching? And that being so, is not the supposed antithesis between the sermon and the devotions of the sanctuary again discovered to be thoroughly misleading and untenable? Is not true preaching worship?

73

I grant you that such a conception of the preacher's task may well overwhelm us with a sense of personal inadequacy and unworthiness. But no lower conception can do justice to the stupendous theme of which we are the heralds. Moreover, the very recognition of preaching as an integral part of worship will save us from many errors. It will restrain us from using the pulpit for the expression of views, preferences and prejudices which are purely personal and subjective. "The pulpit," wrote Bernard Manning, "is no more the minister's than the communion table is his." It will make us resolute to eliminate from our preaching everything that is cheap and showy and meretricious. It will give us a salutary horror of flashy rhetoric, slovenly informality and elegant frippery. It will arm us against the vulgarity of a self-conscious exhibitionism. "No man," declared James Denney, "can give at once the impressions that he himself is clever and that Jesus Christ is mighty to save." Above all, it will inspire us to make our preaching "a living sacrifice, which is our reasonable service." It will drive us to our knees. It will baptize every sermon in the spirit of importunate prayer. Then preaching will be worship indeed.

III

We have seen that the apostolic *kerygma* which at the first carried the Gospel like fire across the world centred in two historic events. To the supreme facts of the Cross and the Resurrection, which are really not two but one, our preaching must ever return, and from them it must continually derive fresh strength and urgency and inspiration.

"I, if I be lifted up from the earth, will draw all men unto Me." There is no magnetism like that. Show men Calvary "towering o'er the wrecks of time," and you will not preach in vain. Incomparably the greatest service you can ever perform for those committed to your charge is to thrust the Cross before their eyes. Leave this out, and all your other appeals and exhortations will be as nothing: empty, useless, unsubstantial words. Set this at the centre, and it will prove itself to be, in the twentieth century as in the first, the power of God unto salvation.

Now the herald of the Cross has a twofold task. He must present his theme in a double setting. On the one hand, he must preach the Cross *in the context of the world's suffering*. Your own congregation will be a microcosm of humanity; and for many of those to whom you minister, the dark mystery which has haunted the sons of men from the dawn of time will be no abstract, impersonal problem to be academically explained, but a grim reality to be faced and fought. Be very clear about this, that what men and women need, face to face with the mystery of pain and trouble and tragedy, is not a solution that will satisfy the intellect, not that primarily at any rate, but a force that will stabilize the soul; not a convincing and coercive argument as to the origins of evil or the reasons why such suffering is permitted on the earth, but a power

75

that will enable them to "stand in the evil day, and having done all, to stand": in short, not an explanation, but a victory.

Right down in the heart of this situation you are to set the Cross. You may, indeed, lead up to the great light that breaks from Calvary by calling attention to certain gleams that pierce the darkness of the way. For example, you will surely be constrained to show that much of what men suffer is but the other side, the necessary correlative, of the immense gain and privilege of living in a world where law and not caprice holds sway; that those who accept the assets of corporate membership in the human family must also be prepared to accept its liabilities; that any system which guaranteed preferential treatment to the righteous and immunity from trouble to the unoffending would in point of fact corrupt the very ethic that it seemed to stablish and support; that in any case man demands danger, and thrives on hazard, and wants no lotus-land of ghastly ease; above all, that it is possible to use trouble creatively, transmuting pain into power and sorrow into love, so that in the end such trouble positively adds on to life's total experience, instead of negatively subtracting from it. All this may rightly enter into the message by which you seek to reinforce faith and to rally the courage in the depths of sorely burdened hearts. Nor will you lack vivid illustration of the thrilling truth that the worst sufferings may be the raw material of character and Christlike loveliness of soul.

Yet I should pity the man who has to stand and face
a congregation with no surer word than that. And I
would implore you not to mock the bitterness of human
hearts with facile phrases about the nobility of pain,
nor to invade with well-meaning platitudes the holy
ground where angels fear to tread. There are experiences—desolating experiences of calamity, of wrecked
homes and shattered dreams, of frantic pain, of the
tragic and apparently senseless waste of precious lives
—in the face of which the most rational and philo-
sophical interpretation and even the best theistic
theories must sound hollow and irrelevant. It were
better, if there is no clearer light to give, to be silent
altogether in the presence of the ultimate mystery; or
else to leave with those who suffer the immeasurably
poignant message of one who died some twenty years
before Christ was born: "O passi graviora, dabit deus
his quoque finem."

But the least in the Kingdom of God is greater than
Vergil when he penned that mighty line. For we have
seen the Cross. We have found the clue to the enigma.
Long ago there was a prophet who, bewildered by the
ways of Providence and appalled by the grim and
harrowing aspect of the world, took counsel with his
soul and made a high resolve: "I will stand upon my
watch-tower, and set me upon the outlook-turret, and
will watch to see what He will say unto me." And a
great part of our task as preachers is to help others,
battered and besieged by the assaults of doubt, to
climb to that high rampart above the dust and smoke

and tumult, the watch-tower of Mount Calvary. For there the new perspective is given which makes men more than conquerors. None of our poor human explanations of life's dark mystery can heal the hurt of baffled and tormented souls. Nothing can suffice but this—to see Love Incarnate taking upon itself the very worst that suffering and evil can do upon the earth, God going into action once for all against the powers of darkness, Christ reigning from the deadly tree, and making His victory there the pledge and the assurance for all the sons of men.

Preach the Cross in the context of the world's suffering, and men will learn, not only that Christ is with them in the dark valley, God "afflicted in all their affliction," gathering up their distress and desolation into His own eternal heart—not only that, though that indeed, even if there were no more to be said, would be a mighty reinforcement: they will learn this other great thing, that God in His sovereign love still leads captivity captive, still transforms the wrecking circumstances of life into means of grace, the dark places into a Holy of Holies, and the thorns that pierce into a crown of glory. For the Cross means that even when things are at their worst, even when life does not bear thinking about, God is master of the situation still, and nothing can spoil His final pattern or defeat His purpose of love.

I would point out that this is a Gospel you can preach without any fear of sentimentalism. There is always a danger that the longing to help the troubled and to bind up the broken-hearted may lead to a preaching of the wrong kind of comfort. There is a type of consolation which tends to romanticize the burden of the mystery, and to interpose religion as a cushion against the blows of fate. Beware of all such expedients: they are far removed from what the New Testament means by comfort. They serve only to hypnotize the troubled mind and to enervate the soul; and in the end they reduce efficiency for the battle of life. "The noblest specimen in existence," according to Principal W. M. Macgregor, "of the preaching of consolation is found in the First Epistle of Peter." True Gospel comfort never plays down to natural weakness: it lifts up to supernatural strength. There is nothing enfeebling or demoralizing about it, no flying to the drug of fantasy: it is essentially virile, bracing, reinforcing. And what gives it this character, preserving it from the risk of sentimentalism, is the Cross at the centre of it. In the last resort, the human heart is too big to find its comfort in any soothing anodyne of consolatory words. There is no comfort short of victory. And it is this, nothing less, that the preacher of the Gospel is empowered to offer to all who turn their faces to the Cross —the comfort of mastering every dark situation, and triumphing in every tribulation, through the grace of Him who conquered there.

IV

But the herald of the Cross has a further task. He must present his theme, not only in the setting of human suffering, but also *in the context of the world's sin*. He will not allow any superficial appearances of complacence to deceive him. For he knows that all history is the record of man's age-long desperate endeavour to answer the dilemma of moral failure and defeat. He knows that God is sending him to people wrestling with the same stubborn predicament. He knows the secret struggles, frustrations and contradictions of his own soul. He dare not on this matter be hesitant or ambiguous. His preaching will never really touch a single heart unless it brings some sure word about sin and its forgiveness.

There have been, indeed, certain classical answers to the dilemma, to which men cling pathetically even to-day. There is the answer of the Jew: over against the guilt and power of sin, the Jew sets the sacrificial system and the efficacy of an elaborate cult. There is the answer of the Greek: it was characteristic of the Greek mind, with its double allegiance to art and philosophy, that it believed man could work out his own salvation aesthetically and intellectually. There is the answer of the Roman: law and order would redeem the race from disintegration, moralism and lisciplined conduct would guarantee the soul. These three historic answers to the human dilemma have made their way right down the centuries, resurrecting themselves in every new generation. Multitudes of our fellow-men—and some of those to whom you will preach—have no other creed to-day. Religious observance and the due performance of ritual acts, the development of culture and the application of logic and intelligence, the natural virtues of the human heart and the attention to good works—what more, it is asked, does man require for his deliverance? But our age, perhaps more than any of its predecessors, is being visited by doubts. It suspects that the malady is too radical to yield to any of these expedients. It has had such an appalling insight into what the apostle called "the mystery of iniquity" that its poise and confidence have been irreparably disturbed. It dare not face a future in which man is his own redeemer.

Wherefore God be thanked that right down in the heart of that situation you can set the Cross! Rising out of the midnight of man's despair, smiting the darkness like a sudden dawn, comes the solving word, the divine decisive deed; and all the classic answers of Jew and Greek and Roman fade away before the glory of it.

Now when you set the Cross in the context of the world's sin, there will be three main notes in your preaching.

You will preach the Cross, first, as *Revelation*. Where else does the terrible truth about sin stand so nakedly revealed as at the place where it crucifies the Son of God? All the habitual rationalizations which reduce sin to ignorance, or biological maladjustment, a thing to be cured by education, social planning or psychological suggestion, are seen at Calvary to be bland distortions of the truth. Let your preaching of the Cross drive home the fact that the same sins which put Christ there are rampant in the world to-day; that it was no monstrous eruption of iniquity that perpetrated the deed of Calvary, but familiar, common things like pride and cowardice and apathy and self-seeking which make their dwelling in the hearts of all; and that these things, rooted in our own lives, working themselves out eventually on the scale of society and gathering themselves up into the collective evil of the world, still crucify the Lord of glory. "Why persecutest thou Me?"

Moreover, you will hold up the Cross as a revelation, not only of the hatefulness of sin, but also of the divine judgment upon it. For on the day when Christ died at its hands, rather than submit or come to terms, He showed once for all what God's mind is about sin to all eternity. Here the divine uncompromising antagonism was irrevocably proclaimed. No way of dealing with sin which blurred the moral issue could be tolerated; for otherwise the chaos on the earth, so far from being removed, would have been intensified, and there would now have been added to it chaos in heaven as well. Before sin could be overcome, it must be judged. And Christ, by resisting it unto blood, has pronounced its utter condemnation. God has judged it for ever.

But greatest of all the paradoxes you will have to preach is this—that the same event which unveils evil in its terrifying, demonic malignity reveals also invincible love. That God should have taken the most awful triumph of naked, unmitigated iniquity, and made precisely *that* the vehicle for the supreme revelation of Himself—here surely is a marvel that beggars description: here is the ultimate hope of our sin-tormented world. You do not preach the Cross aright until you make men hear, on the lips of the Crucified, such words as Joseph spoke to his betrayers: "So now it was not you who sent me hither, but God." Call the Cross the nefarious deed of Annas, Caiaphas and Pilate, call it the supreme revelation of the inmost essence of sin, call it the act of our own contemporary society or (in Pauline phrase) of "the potentates of the dark present, the spirit-forces of evil"—and you will tell the truth, but not the whole truth, not the final and decisive truth. Call it the act of God, call it the mightiest of all His mighty acts, call it the point in history where love divine was supremely master of the situation—and the deeper truth will begin to emerge. You will be helping men to realize that the most desperate chaos sin can perpetrate to-day is not too grim for this amazing love to handle and transform. And through your preaching—please God—they will understand in a new and living way the magnificent outburst of the apostle: "He that spared not His own Son, but delivered Him up for us all, how shall He not with Him also freely give us all things?"

This leads me to the second note in your preaching of the Cross. Preach it as *Victory*. If you speak of Calvary only in terms of revelation, you may be gaining the approval of the opponents of a "transactional theology," but you are certainly diluting disastrously the faith of the New Testament. No Pentecost will ever attend a ministry which boggles at the implications of Christ's cry upon the Cross, "It is finished!" For something happened then which settled the issue for ever. "Once and for all"—that is the authentic trumpet-note of apostolic religion. "I beheld Satan as lightning fall from heaven." That is decisive. After Calvary, it can never be midnight again. Long and hard may be the campaign: for "we wrestle against principalities and powers." But we know now that we are fighting a defeated enemy. "Christ died for our sins," says Peter in his epistle, "the just for the unjust, once for all." "In that He died," writes Paul to the Romans, "He died for sin, once for all." "He has appeared," declares the epistle to the Hebrews, "once for all to abolish sin by the sacrifice of Himself." By all means, drop the word "transaction" if you please: no doubt the term has been abused. But do not mutilate the Gospel of the Cross by reducing it to a doctrine of subjective influence. Preach the Cross as victory. Here where the very greatness of the apparent triumph of iniquity was its own irrevocable defeat; here where evil once for all has shot its bolt, and its deadly weapon is turned against itself; here where eternal love is seen asserting its sovereignty, not just in spite of the tragic mystery of sin, but—as by a master-stroke of divine strategy—precisely through that mystery—here is the ground of all our hope. Here the human prospect has been transfigured radically and for ever.

Preach the Cross, then, as God's all-sufficient answer to man's perpetual question, "How can I win salvation? How can I achieve self-conquest?" There are people in all our congregations to-day asking that question, just as Saul of Tarsus asked it in the lecture-room of Gamaliel, as Luther asked it in the monastery at Erfurt, as John Wesley asked it in the Holy Club at Oxford. Laboriously these men hewed out (to use Jeremiah's figure) their broken cisterns, toiling to store up their good works and creditable achievements, their charities, austerities and penances. But for Saul and Luther and Wesley the day came when their question "How shall I win salvation?" was answered from the throne of God. And the answer was, "You can't! Take it at the Cross for nothing, or not at all." "I have gotten me Christ," cried Donald Cargill in the hour of his execution, "and Christ hath gotten me the victory!"

But it is the whole human situation, not simply the plight of the individual, which the Cross transforms. Let no one, listening to your preaching, have any doubt that when we Christians say that the dark demonic powers which leave their dreadful trail of devastation across the world are ultimately less powerful than Jesus, we really mean it—just as the early disciples meant it when they declared that Christ had raided the realm of Satan and broken the fast-bound chains of hell. If there are professing Christians to-day who do not see the relevance of the Gospel to the desperate situation of this tortured world, it can only be because there is still a veil upon their hearts when they stand at Calvary. It is for you to show them the Cross as it truly is—Christ in action, victor over death, vanquisher of the demons, going forth conquering and to conquer.

Finally, your preaching of the Cross, having struck the notes of Revelation and Victory, will include the note of *Challenge*. Our own hearts bear witness that there is nothing like the Cross of Jesus to shame our selfishness, to abase our pride of intellect, to rebuke our false ambitions, and to bring to birth within us a passionate longing that our lives might reveal something of the spirit which shone so gloriously in His. No doubt, as Bernard Manning has argued, it is a weakness of Cardinal Newman's great hymn "Praise to the Holiest in the height" that after the strong, pungent theology of the earlier verses the penultimate stanza descends to anti-climax—"humanitarian tinkling," Manning calls it:

> And in the garden secretly,
> And on the Cross on high,
> Should teach His brethren, and inspire
> To suffer and to die.

The sacrifice of the God-Man was infinitely more, as we have seen, than an example of gallantry and fortitude, a lesson to humanity how to suffer and die. Nevertheless, the element of challenge persists: and in every soul out of which the sense of nonour and chivalry has not died the Cross lets loose a cleansing tide of penitence and hope, and creates a motive stronger even than the instinct of self-preservation. Lead men straight to Calvary, if you would bind them to Christ's allegiance with the unbreakable fetters which alone give perfect freedom. "He died for us that, whether we wake or sleep, we should live together with Him."

v

But now let me raise a question. What is the most characteristic word of the Christian religion? Suppose you were asked to single out one word to carry and convey the cardinal truth of the Gospel, what word would you choose? I suggest it would have to be the word Resurrection. That is what Christianity essentially is—a religion of Resurrection. Go back and listen to the preachers of the early Church. They never pointed men to the Cross without showing them the Resurrection light breaking behind it. Even when, like Paul, they "determined to know nothing save Jesus Christ and Him crucified," what gave their preaching such grip and converting power was the testimony, implicit in every word, that this same Jesus was alive, and present, and at work in the world. That was the tremendous truth that coloured and conditioned all their thinking. It did not merely give a distinctive accent to their preaching: it throbbed through every word they said. How could it be otherwise? Christ risen and alive was for them the one dominating reality of life and the very centre of the universe. Paul might have put things even more strongly than he did to the Corinthians. "If Christ be not risen," he declared, "then is our preaching vain." He might have added that, without the Resurrection, the voice of the Christian preacher would never have been heard in the land. There was no Christian congregation in that early age which did not recognize itself to be a community of the Resurrection: and there is no hope of revival in the Church to-day until that basic, glorious truth is reasserted and comes back into its own. Far too often we have been inclined to regard the Resurrection as an epilogue to the Gospel, an addendum to the scheme of salvation, a codicil to the divine last will and testament: thereby betraying not only a deficient historic perspective and a singular disregard of the whole tenor of the New Testament, but also a failure in spiritual understanding and an insufficient hold upon the great verities of the faith. This is no appendix to the faith. This *is* the faith. He is risen. The Lord is risen indeed. To preach this is your life-work: and there is no Gospel without it.

Now here let me stress the urgency of showing forth the Resurrection in its dynamic relevance to world-history. The trouble is that many good, devout people have not yet begun to grasp the full range and sweep of the Easter Gospel. Their conception of it is much too narrow and individualistic, too remote from the struggles of humanity. To them the Resurrection means only the escape of Jesus from the grave, the return of the Master to His disciples, the lovely stories of His meetings with Mary, with Peter, with Thomas,

with the two men on the Emmaus road. They have
not gone beyond that, nor seen this event related to the
perpetual conflict of which history is the arena—the
conflict between good and evil, light and darkness, God
and the demons. Therefore I would urge you to
preach the Resurrection as the one fact above all others
which vitally concerns, not only the life of the individual Christian, but the entire human scene and
the destiny of the race. It is the break-through of the
eternal order into this world of suffering and confusion
and sin and death. It is much more than the dramatic
reanimation of One who had died: it is the vindication
of eternal righteousness, the declaration that the heart
of the universe is spiritual. It is the Kingdom of God
made visible. No wonder Paul, meeting the risen
Christ outside Damascus, suddenly fell blinded to the
earth! It was no glare of Syrian sunshine that had
dazzled him. The man had seen, for one tremendous,
piercing moment, the unveiled purpose of God.

Can it be right, then, when our people come up to
God's House on Easter morning, that we should treat
them to reflections on the reawakening of the earth in
springtime, or to a *réchauffé* of the arguments for
immortality? It is a desolating corruption of the
Resurrection Gospel to regard it merely as one more
argument for individual survival. The human heart
indeed cries out for light beyond the grave. All
through your ministry you will hear that cry; and you
will seek, God helping you, to answer it. Nor can you
ever point to any light more clear or steady or reassur-

ing than that which shines from the empty tomb of
Jesus. But I do beseech you to let men see the Easter
hope destroying not only the fear of death, but every
other fear besides, and very specially the fear of the
principalities and powers and wicked forces that corrupt
human nature and fill the earth with ruin. I beg you
to swing the Resurrection light not only over the dim
shadows of the narrow grave, but over the thick darkness of the whole wide world. For the Resurrection
was, and is, the sign of God's unshakable determination
to make Christ Lord of all. The concentrated might
of arrogant iniquity is puny and pathetic and impotent
against the power that took Jesus out of the grave.
This was the conviction which at the first launched
Christianity like a thunderbolt upon the world, and
made its ambassadors superbly fearless. This is the
certainty which burns undimmed in every truly Christian heart to-day. The power which went into action
in the raising again of Jesus will never, through the
darkest of dark ages, fail nor be discouraged: one day
it will resurrect the world. "This is the Lord's doing,
and it is marvellous in our eyes."

But there is a further fact which makes the high
calling of the preacher of the Resurrection immeasurably thrilling and momentous, and it is this. Christ,
being raised from the dead, is an abiding presence for
ever; and you, the preachers of the Resurrection, are
not only the heralds of a historic event, but also the
mediators of a living presence. This is no exaggerated
cliché of a nebulous mysticism: it is a strictly accurate,

unrhetorical statement of fact. You remember Wordsworth's plaintive cry to the shade of Milton, whose
mighty voice had long since ceased to speak:

> Milton! thou shouldst be living at this hour:
> England hath need of thee: she is a fen
> Of stagnant waters.

But if men, looking out upon the stricken human scene
to-day, are fain to cry, "Christ, Thou shouldst be
living at this hour: the world hath need of Thee!"—
back comes the answer with a thousand trumpets in it,
"Should be? He is!" "I am He that liveth, and
was dead; and, behold, I am alive for evermore."
And you, the commissioned servants of the Lord of
the Resurrection, are to tell men that the same Jesus
who was with Latimer and Ridley in the fire, with
Margaret Wilson tied to a stake on the Solway Sands,
with Bunyan in prison, with Gordon in Khartoum,
with Shackleton on the great ice-barrier, with Paul in
the wilds of Asia, with John in the convict-mines of
Patmos, with Peter in the Roman arena—that this
same Jesus still travels through the world in the greatness of His strength, mighty to save, still meets the
troubled heart with the divine promise, "Lo, as I was
with all those others, so will I be with thee!" Nothing
else your ministry may achieve will be of much account
unless you show men that Christ, and get their eyes
open to the real presence of the risen Lord. If in the
grace of God you can do that, they will bless you for it,
and the power of the Spirit will go through the Church
again: and hearts will burn with that authentic fire

without which all altars are cold and all worship dead.

Need I add that the first essential is that your own life should be possessed utterly by the truth and the glory of the Resurrection Gospel? Perhaps the vitalizing of many a ministry waits upon some such experience as that which came to R. W. Dale. The story is familiar—how one day when he was engaged upon writing an Easter sermon for his people the reality of the all-but-incredible fact broke in upon him as it had never done before. "Christ is alive," he found himself crying, "alive! Living as really as I myself am! It came upon me as a burst of sudden glory. Christ is living! My people shall know it." It may not come to us—the great heart-piercing conviction—in any such dramatic way: but if not, then come in some more secret way it must, or we have no awakening Gospel to preach. Pray God that the truth of the Resurrection may smite you with its glory, and go through your mind and spirit with its consuming flame! Only so will you be able to lead others out of the torpor of vague half-belief to the vitality of passionate conviction. John Keats said of his poem *Lamia* that it had "that sort of fire in it that must take hold of people some way"; and of Christian preaching the same claim should be true. Too often in our churches we are still on the wrong side of Easter. We are like the groping, fumbling disciples between Good Friday and the Resurrection. How our congregations would worship, with what joy and eagerness and abandon the sacrifice of praise would rise to God, if all worshippers knew themselves in very truth to be sons and daughters of the Resurrection!

Alfred Noyes has a striking poem, *The Lord of Misrule*, which confronts us with the challenging thought that if the facts of our holy religion and our supernatural faith no longer move us to exultation, then the pagan world itself will rise up and condemn us—that pagan world which revels in the lesser gifts of nature. The poem is based on the tradition reported by an old Puritan writer that "on May-days the wild heads of the parish would choose a Lord of Misrule, whom they would follow even into the Church, though the minister were at prayer or preaching, dancing and swinging their may-boughs about."

> Come up, come in with streamers!
> Come in, with boughs of may!
> Now by the gold upon your toe
> You walked the primrose way.
> Come up, with white and crimson!
> O, shake your bells and sing;
> Let the porch bend, the pillars bow,
> Before our Lord, the Spring!

Then into the pulpit itself, where a few moments before the preacher had been droning his drowsy flock to sleep, the Lord of Misrule pushes his way, and faces the congregation:

> "You chatter in Church like jackdaws,
> Words that would wake the dead,
> Were there one breath of life in you,
> One drop of blood," he said.

Finally, the organ itself takes up the challenge:

> 'Come up with blood-red streamers.'
> The reeds began the strain.
> The *vox humana* pealed on high,
> 'The spring is risen again!'
> The *vox angelica* replied—'The shadows flee away!
> Our house-beams were of cedar.   Come in, with boughs
> of may!'
> The *diapason* deepened it—'Before the darkness fall,
> We tell you He is risen again!
> Our God hath burst His prison again!
> The Lord of Life is risen again; and Love is Lord of all.'

So out of the mouth of paganism itself our dull loss of wonder is judged and our half-belief stands condemned. For if the rebirth of nature is a theme for shouts of joy, how much more the rising from the dead of a Saviour God!   And if we, the children of the Resurrection, should hold our peace, would not the stones immediately cry out?

Make it, then, the goal of your endeavour to help others to discover, or to rediscover, the magnificence of their Christian heritage.   The splendour of the Resurrection Gospel baffles speech, and breaks through language and escapes.   But there is a Spirit who will take our poor, faltering, stammering words, and will work even through these to smite men with the glory of Christ's rising.

VI

One point remains.   Apostolic preaching, as we have already noted, set forth the facts of the Cross and the Resurrection in their organic relationship to the Kingdom of God. In these supreme events, it declared, the Kingdom, long dreamt of and foretold, had now appeared. By this invasion of the supernatural into human experience all life's issues were immeasurably deepened, and the sense of urgency and crisis dramatically intensified. The new era of the Spirit had broken in with power. Until we recapture and restore this apostolic perspective and emphasis, our preaching will be maimed and crippled.

If the trumpet give an uncertain sound on this matter, the whole cause of the Kingdom will suffer. And at no point has there been greater confusion, even amongst Christians. Some have thought of the Kingdom of God as a New Jerusalem for man to build. Some have postponed it to an indefinite future, a far-off divine event in which man has no part. Thus two opposing attitudes have emerged and come into collision: the activism of a thoroughgoing thisworldliness, and the quietism of a thoroughgoing otherworldliness. Your Gospel of the Kingdom must act as a corrective of both these distorted views. To those who stand for the former, it will say: "You are right to bear the world's injustices and oppressions upon your souls, and to go forth against these with the passion of crusaders. You are right to denounce a piety that talks incessantly to men about the bread of heaven, and never stirs a finger to give them bread for their bodies or employment for their energies or decent housing for their families. You are right to insist that

95

if Christianity once turned the world upside down, it can do the same to-day. But you are wrong to disregard the one true source of all strong action and effective power. You are wrong to think the human demand can ever be satisfied with improved communities and garden cities. You are wrong to think that the best economic Paradise will ever still the tumult of a heart that goes crying out for ever for 'a city which hath foundations, whose builder and maker is God '." On the other hand, to those who stand for a predominantly otherworldly quietism, your Gospel of the Kingdom will declare: "You are right to dwell in the secret place of the Most High. You are right to walk with God as pilgrims and sojourners here, looking beyond this transitory scene to the bliss of life eternal. You are right to believe that to God alone belong the Kingdom, the power, and the glory. But you are wrong to lock yourselves up in that secret place of devotion. You are wrong to reduce religion to an unethical, sentimental irrelevance. You are wrong if, in the presence of social misery and injustice, you do not see Christ's eyes blazing like a flame of fire, nor hear His voice, like a trumpet, crying 'I will have mercy, and not sacrifice!'"

It is not within the scope of these Lectures to discuss Christianity and the social order. This only I will say. Carlyle once wrote a letter to Emerson, warning him against a philosophy of spiritual aloofness. "Alas, it is so easy to screw one's self up into high and ever higher altitudes of Transcendentalism, and see nothing under one but the everlasting snows of Himmalayah, the Earth shrinking to a Planet, and the indigo firmament sowing itself with daylight stars; easy for *you*, for me: but whither does it lead? Well, I do believe, for one thing, a man has no right to say to his own generation, turning quite away from it, 'Be damned!' It is the whole Past and the whole Future, this same cotton-spinning, dollar-hunting, canting and shrieking, very wretched generation of ours. Come back into it, I tell you." So too, in your presentation of the great facts of faith, you must resolutely work out the ethical implications of the doctrines you preach. The suspicion that the Church of Christ lacks zeal for social righteousness can be terribly damaging. Nor can it be denied that too often in the past organized religion has tended to play for safety. As Phillips Brooks once put it: "The pillars of the Church are apt to be like the Pillars of Hercules, beyond which no man might sail." It is the function of economists, not of the pulpit, to work out plans of reconstruction. But it is emphatically the function of the pulpit to stab men broad awake to the terrible pity of Jesus, to expose their hearts to the constraint of that divine compassion which haloes the oppressed and the suffering and flames in judgment against every social wrong. Dr. J. S. Whale has put it forcefully and well: "Any present-day theology which has not a revolutionary sociology as part of its implicit logic is not truly Christian." There is no room for a preaching devoid of ethical directness and social passion, in a day when heaven's trumpets sound and the Son of God goes forth to war.

The conclusion of the matter, then, is this, that if you would keep your emphasis right, avoiding extremes on either side, you must continually be returning, in your preaching of the Kingdom, to the insight of the New Testament preachers. In Jesus Christ, they declared, the great new age had broken through into history. It was really and actively present. Those who had tasted its power were living in a transformed world. But not yet was the divine purpose completely fulfilled. Not yet was the human burden of bodily weakness, frustration and death removed. And so, beyond the mighty acts of the Cross and the Resurrection, these men awaited the crowning verification. The drama of history would have a climax and a goal. God Himself would bring in His perfect Kingdom, and make Christ Lord of all.

These things are true. These we believe, and these we preach. We do not minimize the present, when we say Christ is coming again. On the contrary, it is just because we know the divine will must at last be regnant and supreme that we are passionately concerned that it should rule upon the earth here and now. Just because the future belongs to Christ, we preach that now is the accepted time, now is the critical hour for the assertion of His sovereignty in all the affairs of men, now is the day of salvation.

I have spoken to you of our theme as Christian ministers. Who can measure the responsibility of those who are heralds of such tidings? The late Bishop Gore used to give his final charge to candidates on the eve of their ordination in these impressive words: "To-morrow I shall say to you, wilt thou, wilt thou, wilt thou? But there will come a day to you when Another will say to you, hast thou, hast thou, hast thou?" God grant us unwavering fidelity to our high theme, lest we be ashamed to stand at last before the face of the Son of Man.

Chapter III

THE PREACHER'S STUDY

" This excuses no man's ignorance, that is not able to preach seasonably, and to break, and distribute the bread of life according to the emergent necessities of that Congregation, at that time ; Nor it excuses no man's lazinesse, that will not employ his whole time upon his calling ; Nor any man's vain-glory, and ostentation, who having made a Pye of Plums, without meat, offers it to sale in every Market, and having made an Oration of Flowres, and Figures, and Phrases without strength, sings it over in every Pulpit."—John Donne.

ERNEST RAYMOND, novelist and essayist, has described the most impressive sermon he ever heard. In itself, he relates, the sermon was ordinary enough: intellectually negligible, aesthetically ragged. Its construction was faulty, its delivery abominable. Yet its effect was overwhelming. It was during the war of 1914-18. A group of men had gathered in a cellar to hear an Anglo-Catholic father. They went expecting some dry-as-dust theology or perfervid moral exhortation. But what actually happened was quite different. The preacher, sitting down, and staring at the floor or ceiling in search of words—so halting was his speech—spoke of the text, "Come unto Me, all ye that labour and are heavy laden, and I will give you rest." "I think," wrote Raymond, "he spoke for an hour, and not a man of us moved, and most of us were very quiet all that night."

There you have a striking testimony to the power of preaching to mediate the Real Presence of Christ. What matter though all the rules be broken, as long as men are made piercingly aware of Jesus in the midst? It is one thing to learn the technique and mechanics of preaching: it is quite another to preach a sermon which will draw back the veil and make the barriers fall that hide the face of God. If that is not achieved the most careful craftsmanship is worthless; while on the other hand, all mannerisms can be forgiven, all violent infringing of the rules condoned, if there comes—as through the sermon which so moved Raymond and the others that night—some authentic touch of the unseen, some deep subduing sense of the eternal.

"Can I ever forget," wrote Joseph Parker, "the sermon Gilfillan delivered in my pulpit in Manchester? Nothing like it was ever seen under the sun. He took the sermon out of his trouser pocket and laid it in little heaps on the pulpit Bible, and took it up scrap by scrap, and read each at the pulpit lamp as if he were announcing a bazaar or a tea-meeting." You would scarce credit it that any message could survive the handicap of a delivery so execrable. But listen to the words in which Parker goes on to describe the effect produced. "First the shock, then the almost-laugh, then the wonder, then the prayer, then the heart-felt thanks. It was very wonderful, and often beautiful exceedingly." When preaching impels the hearers to prayer, you may be sure that, whatever its defiance of the accepted canons of the art, it is preaching indeed.

The great Thomas Chalmers, as Professor Hugh Watt in a recent study has reminded us, preached with a disconcertingly provincial accent ("the bruising barbarism of his pronunciation," to use Professor Masson's phrase), with an almost total lack of dramatic gesture, tied rigidly to his manuscript, with his finger following the written lines as he read. Yet vast congregations hung breathlessly upon that preaching, and those sermons went like fire through the land. In that very striking account of a spiritual pilgrimage, *A Wanderer's Way*, Dr. Charles Raven has described an incident which occurred during his student days at Cambridge. It was the visit of a well-known preacher at whose methods and message some were inclined to scoff. "The sermon was as an argument puerile," writes Raven, "but the man was aflame, radiating a power of loving that filled his simple words with meaning and with an atmosphere of worship. Here was a man not only passionately convinced of his gospel, but, for whatever the words mean, God-possessed. . . . Here surely was the real Christianity, that had changed the course of human history: if this man were deluded, I should almost be content to share this delusion. The scoffer stayed to pray." Is it not manifest that the ultimate secret of true preaching—the preaching which begets worship and mediates a Presence and wields converting power—is something quite apart from any rules of logical structure or artistic form? "The wind bloweth where it listeth: and thou canst not tell whence and whither."

This is not to say, however, that the craftsmanship of preaching is to be belittled or despised. That would be quite a false deduction from our premises. To argue that, because the message in itself is so all-important, we can afford to ignore the mere form of its presentation, would be arbitrary and wrong-headed. On the contrary, it is precisely because the message entrusted to us is of such paramount importance that we should labour at it night and day, sparing no pains to become skilled in our craft and to make the earthen vessel as worthy as we can of the treasure it contains. St. Paul thanked God for the Corinthians, that they were "enriched in all utterance, and in all knowledge," for it is essential that those who know the truth of Christ should also learn how to set it forth convincingly for others. In this regard, congregations to-day are much more exacting than they were a generation ago. Probably in no small measure this is due—as a recent writer in the *Spectator* suggested—to the influence of Broadcasting House. "If people listen to competent speaking on all kinds of subjects during the week, they will ask for equal competence from the pulpit on Sunday." Slovenly work, careless technique, faulty construction and inarticulate delivery have had their day: they will pass muster no longer. And surely the preacher's task, undertaken at God's command for Christ's dear sake, demands the very best that unremitting toil and care and disciplined technical training can bring to it. "Neither will I offer burnt offerings unto the Lord my God of that which doth cost me nothing."

Beware, however, of any lecturer who——on the Warrack foundation or any other——should announce a course on "How to Preach: By One who Knows." The creature is an impostor! No man knows how to preach. You will have to reckon with this significant, disconcerting fact, that the greatest preachers who have ever lived have confessed themselves poor bunglers to the end, groping after an ideal which has eluded them for ever. When you have been preaching for twenty years, you will be beginning to realize how incalculably much there is to learn. There will be days when the Socratic knowledge of your ignorance will desolate and overwhelm you. Even if Providence should spare you to this work for fifty years, your thought will be, as the gloaming closes in around you, "If only I could start all over again now!" There is no vocation in all the world which has such rewards to offer of deep and satisfying joy. But it is also true that there is no vocation so perpetually humbling to a good man, no task in which failure is so inescapably the fate appointed. How, indeed, could it be otherwise?

> I who have giv'n to Thee my best
> Rejoice Thy word is unexpressed;
> And inexpressible must be
> On this side of Eternity;
> And I with all my travail vast
> Am glad that I must fail at last.
> If I had found the Word complete,
> No glory could I march to meet:

A pilgrim home from pilgrimage!
A soldier with no fight to wage!
But now my powers I still must spend,
And go on failing to the end,
But failing I shall leave behind
Some hints of the Eternal Mind,
And hungry pilgrims, where I went,
May find a broken Sacrament.

I

In any case, take courage! It is right that the vast
difficulty of the task should humble you. It is wrong
that it should paralyse you. When you sit down in
your study to write a sermon, you are not without vital
resources behind you. All your experience of God, all
your acquaintance with life, all your knowledge of
men, all your fellowship with the great minds of the
centuries, will come in then to your aid.

I do not dwell here on the fundamental resource—
your personal, first-hand communion with God. Of
that I hope to speak in a subsequent lecture. But what
of your acquaintance with the world, your knowledge
of your fellows, your understanding of the problems
and vexations that besiege the souls of men? To be
merely bookish and academic is quite fatal. It is a
damaging criticism of any preacher, that he is out of
touch with the actualities of other men's lives, ignorant
of the conditions with which they have to grapple, and
therefore incompetent to speak to their needs or to give
them counsel and guidance for their struggle. There

is no reason why any man's ministry should be crippled by such aloofness and inhumanity. There is every reason why the ambassador of Christ, more than anyone else, should be alert and sensitive to men's difficulties, aspirations, conflicts, bafflements, to their social and economic strains and stresses and insecurities, to their dreams and defeats, heroisms and tragic blunders. Everything that can help you there—all first-hand acquaintance with contemporary conditions, all working knowledge of psychology, all practical experience of living in community—will bring an indispensable contribution to the resources of insight, understanding and sympathy out of which you are to preach. In this connection, let me urge upon you the immense importance of the preacher's work as pastor. Have nothing to do with the foolish suggestion that the two offices might advantageously be severed. Let no specious arguments about the necessity of conserving your energies, or of concentrating on other tasks, organization, committees, and the like, deflect you from your primary duty of knowing the people whom you are sent to serve for Jesus' sake. Above all, I would ask you to consider this paradox. Would you know men better? Then get closer to God! For indeed the only way to understand your brother truly is to see him as God sees him, to look out upon him through the eyes of the great Father of us all.

There is another resource which will come in powerfully to your aid in the preparation of your messages week by week: your fellowship with the great minds of the centuries. No minister of the Gospel has any right to cease to be a student when his College days are done. However burdened he may be in after years with the crowding cares of a large city congregation, however wearing to body, brain and spirit the toils of his twelve hours' day, he must and he can—by resolution, self-discipline, and the grace of God—remain a student to the end. The preacher who closed down his mind ten, twenty, thirty years ago is a tragic figure. Keep alert to what theology is saying. Refresh your soul with the living waters of the spiritual classics. Augustine's *Confessions*, Baxter's *Reformed Pastor*, Pascal's *Thoughts*, William Law's *Serious Call*, Wesley's *Journal*, von Hügel's *Letters*—all these and many more are your rightful heritage: and who could dwell with these and not be "strengthened with might by God's Spirit in the inner man"? Enlarge your range sometimes to include the great enemies of the faith. Be debtor both to the Greeks and to the barbarians. Know what men have said against our holy religion. See how even there God turns the wrath of man to His praise, and the damaging arguments of the sceptics to the greater glory of Christ. Nor will you, if you are wise, neglect literature of a more general kind. You will find that history and biography, science and literary criticism, drama, fiction, poetry—all have some gift to bring for the preparation of your message. Not that you are to direct your reading with a deliberate eye to the garnering of sermon material! That makes for homiletical professionalism. But to have com-

panied with Shakespeare and Plutarch, Tolstoy and
Dickens, Robert Bridges, Chesterton, Eddington,
T. S. Eliot, is to find all your horizons stretched and
widened. Such intercourse will impart new qualities
of breadth, insight, dignity and precision to all your
work. Therefore, in the words of the apostolic injunction, "give attendance to reading."

Need I remind you that when Paul laid that charge
upon Timothy he was thinking supremely of Scripture
reading? "I do not know," exclaimed Spurgeon,
"how my soul would have been kept alive if it had not
been for the searching of Scripture which preaching
has involved." It is your immense privilege that the
very nature of your calling compels you to live daily in
the pages of the Bible. But do not, I beg you, debase
the Word of God by regarding it as a mere hunting-
ground for texts and subjects. Let there be a deeper
constraint behind your Bible study than the feverish
question, "Now what am I going to preach about next
Sunday?" If all our people need the devotional use of
the Bible for their spiritual nourishment and growth in
grace, how much more do we, who have to speak to
them in the Name which is above every name! Nothing
can atone for slackness and indiscipline at this point.
Let us give ourselves day by day to prayerful and
meditative study of the Word, listening to hear what
God the Lord will speak: lest, when we seek to interpret the Scriptures to others, it should have to be said
of us, in the words of the Samaritan which were once
applied to Robert Southey's attempt to interpret the

life and character of Wesley, "Thou hast nothing to draw with, and the well is deep!"

II

Now before proceeding to discuss the practical questions of sermon construction, there are three pleas I wish to make.

The first is a plea for expository preaching. This is one of the greatest needs of the hour. There are rich rewards of human gratitude waiting for the man who can make the Bible come alive. Congregations are sick of dissertations on problems, and essays on aspects of the religious situation: such sermons are indeed no true preaching at all. Men are not wanting to be told our poor views and arguments and ideals. They are emphatically wanting to be told what God has said, and is saying, in His Word. There is no durable satisfaction in anything less than that. Therefore we do wrong when we take a text and read our message into it. Let the Bible speak its own message. Incidentally, this will deliver us from the peril of monotony. The preacher who expounds his own limited stock of ideas becomes deadly wearisome at last. The preacher who expounds the Bible has endless variety at his disposal. For no two texts say exactly the same thing. Every passage has a quite distinctive meaning. It is not the Holy Spirit's way to repeat Himself. If you can write a sermon, and then attach it to any one of half a dozen texts indiscriminately, you would do well to be suspicious of that sermon! Do not be like the preachers Spurgeon describes, who, having announced their text, "touch their hats, as it were, to that part of Scripture, and pass on to fresh woods and pastures new." Open up the riches that the particular text contains. Remember there is something there which occurs nowhere else. Bring to light its buried treasure. Why should we so often find ourselves racking our brains and cudgelling our souls, and producing in the end only some poor disquisition lamentably devoid of any qualities of vivid interest or grip or appeal? It is because we will persist in driving along the path of our own thoughts and preconceptions instead of following where the Bible leads. Give the strength of your ministry to expository preaching, and not only will you always have a hearing, not only will you keep your message fresh and varied, but, in the truest sense, you will be doing the work of an evangelist; and from many of those quiet words of grateful acknowledgment which are amongst the most precious and sacred rewards of any man's ministry, you will know that through the Scriptures God has spoken again, as He spoke to the fathers by the prophets.

The second plea is for a due observance of the Christian Year. Your own personal devotional life stands to gain much, in discipline, vividness and vitality, by active celebration of the great Christian festivals. Moreover, such observance has no small ecumenical value: it is one way of asserting, through all differences and divisions, our essential unity in

Christ. But what mainly concerns us here is its place in preaching. The great landmarks of the Christian Year—Advent, Christmas, Lent, Good Friday, Easter, Whitsunday, Trinity—set us our course, and suggest our basic themes. They compel us to keep close to the fundamental doctrines of the faith. They summon us back from the bypaths where we might be prone to linger, to the great highway of redemption. They ensure that in our preaching we shall constantly be returning to those mighty acts of God which the Church exists to declare. In passing, I would remind you that the true meaning of Christmas can unfold itself only to those who have climbed the slopes of Advent, that the joy of Easter in all its splendour of victory can lay hold only upon those who have watched through Lent and have been with Christ in His passion, and that the power of Pentecost can be fully revealed only to those who, "with one accord in one place," have waited expectantly for the gift from heaven. Throughout these periods of the year, therefore, our preaching ought to be specifically directed, Sunday by Sunday, towards preparing our people in mind and heart for the fresh disclosure of Himself which it is God's will to send. Then indeed the great triumphant festivals of universal Christendom will become high places of the spirit: a mighty means of grace to a people prepared for the Lord.

My third plea is this. Put into your sermon-making the very best you have in you. Stint no toil to achieve clear thought, fit language, true construction, decisive appeal. The late Viscount Grey once confessed to Lord Bryce the difficulty he experienced in composing speeches. "You need not be disturbed," was the answer, "as long as you feel like that. The time to become alarmed is when you find that you can speak quite easily without having anything to say." If you are gifted with facility of utterance, what Coleridge once shrewdly described as "a premature and unnatural dexterity in the combination of words," beware! If it is your lot to stand on "the slippery floor of a popular pulpit"—to use a phrase of Alexander Whyte's—be doubly on your guard. There will be subtle temptations to scamp the work of preparation. You will be tempted to rationalize your other crowding duties into a justification for relaxing the inexorable discipline of your study-desk. If you are not resolute, the very constitution of the Church itself—its intricate machinery of meetings, committees, conferences, organizations—will seem to aid and abet that weaker, slacker self within which is only too glad to escape the travail of lonely wrestling with the Word of God. If the Church cannot, or will not, break through that vicious circle, you must do it for yourself. You are called to speak to men in the name of God. Dare you think lightly of such an undertaking, or of the stern discipline of heart and mind which it involves? "I earnestly beseech you all," wrote Richard Baxter well-nigh three hundred years ago to his brethren in the ministry, "in the name of God, and for the sake of your peoples' souls, that you will not slightly slubber over this work, but do it vigorously and with all your might and make it your great and serious business."

The preparation of two sermons a week, to say nothing of other talks and addresses, is indeed a tremendous task. I would urge you, for your own peace of mind, to systematize your days. Aim at having one sermon finished by Wednesday night, the other by Friday. As far as lies in your power, guard your mornings from interruption. God, says Jeremiah, "rises up early," to send His prophets: on which John Oman comments pithily, "Naturally His prophets should follow His example." "A man in his study in his bedroom slippers, unshaved and in his dressing-gown, is in about as perilous a state for his soul as a man who takes to secret drinking." "These," says Phillips Brooks, "are the race of clerical visionaries who think vast, dim, vague thoughts, and do no work." A lifelike picture! It would probably be agreed that a sermon which cannot be prayed over before it is preached is hardly likely to set the heather on fire, or to bring to any seeking soul "the fulness of the blessing of the gospel of Christ." And can we honestly pray over a bit of scamped work, or any sermon into which we have not cared to put our best? Dr. Sloane Coffin once declared that "the recipe for compounding many a current sermon might be written: 'Take a teaspoonful of weak thought, add water, and serve.' The fact that it is frequently served hot, may enable the concoction to warm the hearers; but it cannot be called nourishing." You will remember how mercilessly

William Cowper pilloried certain preachers of his day whose shoddy sermons belied the dignity of the prophetic vocation and brought it into contempt:

> The things that mount the rostrum with a skip,
> And then skip down again; pronounce a text;
> Cry—hem! and reading what they never wrote,
> Just fifteen minutes, huddle up their work,
> And with a well-bred whisper close the scene!

Overdrawn? No doubt. Yet the race of "clerical visionaries" is not extinct.

Yours is a task, I repeat, which demands and deserves sheer hard work, sweat of brain and discipline of soul. You must not, for example, allow your week's sermon preparation to be at the mercy of moods. You must not wait for the inspired hour before getting under way. Spurgeon indeed urged his students, when deliberating on the right text to choose, to "wait for that elect word, even if you wait till within an hour of the service." It may have been the wise policy for a Spurgeon; but then Spurgeons are few and far between. Ordinary creatures like ourselves will be well advised to follow the less spectacular and dramatic path of plodding diligence and patience. In any case, you will often find it is as you pursue that hard and apparently thankless way that quite suddenly the fire from heaven begins to fall. Speaking of the art of writing, Sir Arthur Quiller-Couch roundly declared that "solid daily practice is the prescription and 'waiting upon inspiration' a lure. These crests only rise

on the back of constant labour." If that is true of
writing in general, it is certainly true of sermon preparation in particular. "Only out of long preparation
can come the truly triumphant flash." If you persist
in waiting for the divine afflatus, you will waste valuable hours which might have been more profitably
spent in making dogged progress with the work, "line
upon line, here a little, and there a little." Anthony
Trollope, in the *Autobiography*, described his own
methods of work. "It had at this time become my
custom to write with my watch before me, and to
require from myself 250 words every quarter of an
hour. I have found that my 250 words have been
forthcoming as regularly as my watch went." We
may feel disposed to deride such a practice as hope-
lessly mechanical. What we regard as our artistic
temperament cries out against it. But let us not be
blind to the wisdom it contains. Certainly we have
little right to preach to others about conquering the
power of moods if our own sermon preparation is
swayed by that tyranny!

Nor must we presume upon the text which runs,
"Take no thought how or what ye shall speak; for it
shall be given you in that same hour." Only textual
vivisection of the worst kind could twist that passage
into meaning that it is a meritorious action to enter the
pulpit unprepared. It is quite a false antithesis which
would set the toil and premeditation of the study over
against guidance by the Holy Spirit. Jesus was refer-
ring to the special grace which would be ministered to

His followers when the hour of emergency leapt upon them, and they were dragged before rulers and governors. The sudden crisis, He assured them, would bring with it a sudden reinforcement. "As thy days, so shall thy strength be." That is manifestly true, in the twentieth century no less than in the first. But when we as preachers count upon the aid of the Holy Spirit to give us utterance, we would do well to reflect that the promise is conditional upon the loyalty of common days. The Spirit of the Lord will be upon us in proportion as our work has been earnest and faithful and ungrudging.

There are, of course, those who would argue that the place of preaching has long been grossly exaggerated. They minimize its value. Long hours of preparation they regard as waste of energy and effort. They are particularly scornful of anything which may be called "popular preaching." This they would exclude as incompatible with the worship of God. Moreover, they say, its very popularity proves that it is riddled with insincerity. Preaching—"mere" preaching, as the derogatory phrase expresses it—has had its day: let us be finished with the cult of preaching, or at least reduce it to a quite subsidiary place. Let those hours in the study be devoted to more profitable and practical ends! But the pulpit need not fear the battery of such superior critics. It is likely to outlive them all. William Cowper, speaking of the pulpit in that same poem, *The Task*, from which I have already quoted, confesses:

I name it filled
With solemn awe, that bids me well beware
With what intent I touch that holy thing;

and he prophesies that it

Must stand acknowledged, while the world shall stand.

Indeed, as I pointed out in an earlier lecture, the
fashion of disparaging preaching is simply due to
muddled thinking.   It represents a failure to understand what preaching essentially is—the heralding of
the eternal Word of God—and a consequent inability
to grasp its integral place in all true worship.   Nor
should we be misled by any strictures on "popular"
preaching.   To aim at a cheap popularity would indeed
be a despicable disloyalty.   But does it not stand
written of our Lord that "the common people heard
Him gladly"?   John Kelman was a popular preacher:
and there are scores of men to-day who would confess
that it was to Kelman, under God, that they owe their
souls.   Studdert-Kennedy was a popular preacher:
and Studdert-Kennedy did far more to stir the social
conscience of the country than any of the critics who
label popular preaching as dope.   This disparaging of
preaching is a passing phase.   Do not be misled by it.
Resist the suggestion that to sweat blood over your
sermon preparation is a subtle form of pride and selfishness, or at the least a reprehensible misdirection of time
and energy.   Long after all such pontifical utterances
of a one-eyed dogmatism have passed away, it will still

be pleasing God by the foolishness of preaching to save them that believe.

There is no short-cut to escape the burden and the toil. Any evasion of the cost will inevitably rob a man's ministry of power. Any refusal to accept the relentless, implacable discipline will result in diminished spiritual influence. Put into your sermons your unstinting best. When Carlyle was toiling at his *French Revolution*, he wrote to Emerson: "That beggarly Book hampers me every way. To fling it once for all into the fire were perhaps the best; yet I grudge to do that. It is impossible for you to figure what mood I am in. One sole thought. That Book! that weary Book! occupies me continually. For the present, really, it is like a Nessus' shirt, burning you into madness; nay, it is also like a kind of Panoply, rendering you invulnerable, insensible, to all *other* mischiefs." Surely we, who have to wrestle with the Word of truth for the immortal souls of men, must ask no easier way. "What," cries Richard Baxter, "have we our time and strength for, but to lay both out for God? What is a candle made for, but to be burnt?"

III

It may be well at this point to underline two guiding principles which the preacher must constantly keep in sight.

Remember, first, that what you are hoping to produce is a sermon—not an essay, not a lecture, not a

College exegesis, but a sermon. That is to say, when you sit down to write in your study, you must visualize a gathered congregation. This will give your work those qualities of directness, liveliness, verve and immediacy which are so essential. It will prune drastically your involved, elaborate periods, and sternly repress any addiction to purple passages. It will eliminate irrelevances. It will constrain you to clarify your own ideas. It will urge you to translate abstractions into concrete terms. It will embolden you to use personal forms of address. It will banish the dull stilted tediousness of the sermon-essay. It will keep the dominant notes of urgency and reality, of appeal for a verdict, sounding unmistakably. Roman oratory of the classical age had three rules: *placere, docere, movere*. To please, in the sense of gripping the hearers' minds and keeping interest alert; to teach and instruct, as distinct from the purveying merely of exhortation and uplift, and the recital of pious platitudes; to move the heart, and sting the will into action—is not this the Christian preacher's task? And where is the possibility of its accomplishment unless there stands vividly before his consciousness, as he prepares his sermon in his study, the vision of his waiting congregation, the thought of the men and women, with all their crowding, clamorous needs, to whom as Christ's ambassador he is to speak?

In this connection, let me draw your attention to a striking passage in Jebb's Lectures on *The Growth and Influence of Classical Greek Poetry*, in which the Greek poet and the Christian preacher are compared. The paragraph is well worth pondering. "In every province of intellectual activity, and in that of poetry among the rest, the Greeks of the classical age demanded a living sympathy of mind with mind. What they felt in regard to the poet can be best understood by comparing it with the feeling which not they alone, but all people, have in regard to the orator and the preacher. The true orator, the great preacher, speaks out of the fulness of genuine conviction and emotion to the minds and hearts of those who hear him; through all variations of mood and tone, he keeps in mental touch with them. The excellence of the classical Greek poet was tried by the same test. No elaboration of art could sustain the poet through his ordeal, if he failed in truth to nature. False sentiment may pass muster in the study, but it is inevitably betrayed by its own unveracity when it is spoken aloud before listeners whose minds are sane, as those of the Greeks preeminently were; the hollow ring is detected; it offends; and the exemption of the best Greek poetry from false sentiment is a merit secured by the very conditions under which that poetry was produced." Remember, therefore, to keep your congregation before you as you write. For no array of literary merits can possibly redeem a discourse which lacks the living sympathy of mind with mind.

The other basic principle is this. Make sure that every sermon you preach has a definite aim. To say this is indeed simply to apply in one particular and very important direction a truth which ought to govern a man's whole ministry. Why are we in this work at all? To bring men to God through Jesus Christ. That is the ultimate goal of all our striving, the purpose of our commission. It ought to be our one consuming ambition to help men and women, through the services of the sanctuary, to meet the living God. And if ever we lose sight of that commanding goal, if we grow hazy and uncertain about our aim, if we eventually reach a point where we have ceased expecting the Holy Spirit to act mightily amongst our people with convincing and converting power, the Lord have mercy on our souls! "Why should it be thought a thing incredible that God should raise the dead"—yes, even through our poor preaching? Therefore, as our whole ministry must press toward that mark, as it can have meaning and value and momentum only by keeping that goal in sight, so every sermon must have its own quite definite aim. "A sermon," said Beecher, "is not like a Chinese fire-cracker to be fired off for the noise which it makes. It is the hunter's gun, and at every discharge he should look to see his game fall." There is something wrong with a preacher who sends people away with the bemused and puzzled feeling, "Now what was all that about? What was the fellow driving at to-day?" The artist in *Don Quixote*, on being interrogated what precisely he was painting, replied, "That is as it may turn out." Who has not suffered under sermons evolved in the same deplorably haphazard way? The acid test is to confront yourself, before ever

What next? The immediate step is to set down on paper—without any regard at this stage for logical sequence—all the thoughts, suggestions, illustrations which your chosen theme brings clustering into your mind. Do not let the resultant disarray and confusion unduly daunt you! However chaotic that page, go ahead: get everything down. That done, your next undertaking is to reduce the chaos to order. Out of that jumbled mass of material you are to hammer a coherent shape. Now here I would urge you to spare no pains. Clarity, logical progression, natural transitions, closely riveted connections—these are duties you owe to your hearers. The preacher who stints toil at this point, being disinclined for the strenuous mental discipline involved, is laying upon his congregation the onus of a task which is really his, not theirs. He is transferring to them a burden he ought to have taken on himself. Is it surprising that their acceptance of it should, to put it mildly, lack enthusiasm? Never grudge the labour which clear thinking and methodical construction demand. A sermon which has some symmetry about it, built to an orderly plan and showing evidence of carefully chiselled thought, is likely to have far more thrust and grip and attack upon the hearers' minds than any amorphous collection of fine ideas. There is a story of a young minister who, concerned about the apparent failure of his preaching, consulted Dr. Joseph Parker in the vestry of the City Temple. His sermons, he complained, were encountering only apathy. Could Dr. Parker frankly tell him what was lacking? "Suppose you preach me one of your sermons here and now," said Parker; and his visitor, not without some trepidation, complied. When it was over, the Doctor told him to sit down. "Young man," he said, "you asked me to be frank. I think I can tell you what is the matter. For the last half-hour you have been trying to get something out of your head instead of something into mine!" That distinction is crucial. Wrestle with your subject in the study, that there may be clarity in the pulpit. "For if the trumpet give an uncertain sound, who shall prepare himself to the battle?"

Now comes the actual writing of the sermon. Immediately the question confronts you, How to begin? It was the almost invariable habit of the preachers of a bygone generation, having announced a text, to start off by expounding its Scripture setting and historical background. Nor is this method by any means to be despised to-day. For one thing, it provides a corrective of that arbitrary treatment of Scripture which, breaking all the canons of exegesis, imports meanings into texts in complete disregard of what the original writer meant to say. For another thing, the historical setting, if briefly and vividly sketched, will illuminate and make doubly relevant the message of the text itself. Thus, for example, a sermon on Zechariah's young man with the measuring-line might well begin with some account of the danger which the prophet sensed in the rebuilding of Jerusalem—the danger, namely, that the new community might be constructed precisely upon the

lines of the old, a facsimile of the city that had stood
there before the divine judgments in history had swept
it away. Is that not a real peril still, that men should
have their faces to the past rather than to the future,
hankering after the social structure or the economic
security or the ecclesiastical divisions which their
fathers knew? Or again, if you have decided to preach
on Isaiah's "Watchman, what of the night?" you
might not unfittingly introduce your subject by showing that the watchman is one of the great figures of
Scripture, to be descried on page after page, standing
on the walls of beleaguered cities, peering through the
darkness infested by foes, scanning the horizons for
the coming of a deliverer, keeping vigil (as the apostle
saw him) over troubled hearts like the sentinel peace
of God. Given the saving grace of brevity, and some
faculty of historical imagination, much is to be said for
the recognized tradition of starting from the Scripture
context, and working on from that to the message for
to-day.

There is, however, another method which is better
adapted to grip your hearers' attention and secure their
interest at the very outset, especially in these days
when so many of them have the notion—the quite
erroneous but stubbornly prevalent notion—that the
world of the Bible is remote and alien from their own.
This is to start from present-day experience. Begin
where your hearers are. Meet them on their own
ground. Let us assume, for example, that you are
going to preach a sermon on the conquest of depres-

sion, taking for your text the words in 1 Samuel, "David encouraged himself in the Lord his God." Instead of starting with a historical introduction based on the Biblical incident, go straight to the experience of your hearers themselves. Your first sentences will arrest their attention, if you speak of the disheartened moods which no one quite escapes, and of those difficult days when work is a weariness and resilience is low, or when life has defeated some cherished hope and dreams have died. Then ask them to observe how one brave spirit faced this very test and emerged victorious. Show them David, as that most moving page of Old Testament biography depicts him, girding himself to meet a succession of adversities that might well have made any man a nervous wreck. Not by the method of the Stoic, who lectures his own soul on the matter of morale; not by the way of the wishful thinker, who practises a comfortable self-deception; not by these did this man triumph, but by letting God in upon the situation, by an act of religious realism that smote the low mood and brought dawn breaking through the midnight of the soul. Or again, suppose your subject is Handicapped Lives, and your text Paul's thorn in the flesh. If you begin with a disquisition on the apostle's disability, your hearers may accord you only that tepid interest which a doubtfully relevant theme elicits. But start off from the fact that almost every life is conscious of a handicap of some kind—whether of health, or talent, or opportunity, or personality, or social gift—and immediately their attention is engaged:

for you will be touching the very nerve of their own experience. Then you will go on to show how Paul, by the grace of Christ, turned his limitations to glorious gain, and how any man or woman to-day may do the same.

A useful variant of this method of approach is to begin with some arresting incident or picture from life or literature. Take, for instance, a subject on which you are bound to speak to your people not once but many times, the immemorial question "Does God care?" You might prelude your sermon on this theme with that extraordinarily vivid picture Carlyle gives near the beginning of *Sartor*—the philosopher gazing out across the city at midnight from his lofty attic, musing on the mingled joys and sorrows, hopes and miseries of the half-a-million human beings huddled round him there: "But I," he exclaims at last, "I sit above it all; I am alone with the Stars." Is God like that—an aloof, spectator God? Or you might begin with that youthful outburst in one of Hugh Walpole's stories. "You know that there can't be a God, Vanessa. In your heart you must know it. You are a wise woman. You read and think. Well, then, ask yourself: How *can* there be a God and life be as it is?" The great initial advantage of this method is that it vivifies the crucial issue with which you are proposing to deal. Right at the outset in a couple of sentences or little more—as in the vivid strokes of a lightning artist—it focuses the dramatic relevance of the theme, and thrusts it compellingly upon mind and heart.

It will not have escaped your notice, in this connection, how often our Lord Himself in His teaching found His point of departure in some incident, scene or inquiry uppermost in His hearers' minds at the moment. Instead of beginning with an exposition of the fundamental verities of religious faith, He would begin with the concrete stuff of life, the raw material of familiar experience; and thence would lead on and up to the eternal truth it was His mission to declare. Jesus got His texts, time and again, from the congregations gathered around Him. So, too, with St. Paul at Athens. "As I passed by, I found an altar 'To the Unknown God.'" That arrested attention immediately. That nailed down the issue, fastening it firmly to contemporary fact. Rightly and wisely, the apostle began just where his hearers were, hoping that as his argument marched to its climax he would be able to lead them through to an acceptance of the ultimate revelation in Christ. Let me add that the trouble about that Athenian sermon was, not that he began there, but that he stayed there too long. The blunder was—and mark this well, for it is a common fault with preachers still—that half his discourse that day was introduction. Indeed, it was only at the end that the trumpet-note of God's mighty act in Christ was heard. Perhaps Paul on Mars' Hill was conscious of a latent antagonism in his congregation. Perhaps his surprising adoption of alien methods—rhetoric and philosophy, classical allusions and bits of poetry—was a deliberate peace-offering intended to neutralize the unspoken criticisms with which the atmosphere seemed sultry. At all events, reflecting subsequently on the comparative failure of that sermon, he resolved that never again would he lengthen out his prologue so discursively, nor travel to his goal by so roundabout a road. Between Athens and Corinth, the decision was reached. He would indeed meet his hearers on their own ground, but he would take them straight from there to Jesus Christ, crucified and risen. Well for us if we have learnt the same lesson, and made the same vow in our own souls! If you have a propensity towards long and involved introductions, check it ruthlessly. A few vivid sentences can be so much stronger and more telling than the most elaborate historical or theological approach. "Gentlemen," said Spurgeon to his students, "don't go creeping into your subject, as some swimmers go into the water, first to the ankles, and then to the knees, and then to the waist and shoulders: plunge into it at once over head and ears!"

Before passing from this matter, let me add that perhaps the ideal sermon introduction is that which consists in a judicious combination of the two main methods outlined above. One example must suffice. Take the striking incident of Paul's encounter at Ephesus with the group of disciples who had never "so much as heard whether there be any Holy Ghost." A sermon on this text might begin from the Biblical passage itself. You might portray Paul puzzling over the lack of vitality and the sense of strain in the religious life of those Ephesian converts, until the root of the trouble was disclosed; and then you would draw the parallel with that desupernaturalized Christianity so familar to-day, which awaits a fresh baptism of power. Or alternatively, your sermon might set out from the contemporary situation, from the manifest failure of the Christian forces to make their God-intended impact upon this generation, and from the disturbing question haunting so many hearts, "Why has my religion not made a more vital difference to me?" Then you would ask your hearers to observe the Word of God confronting this precise perplexity, diagnosing the trouble with sure insight, and dealing with it decisively. But better than either of these lines of approach to the cardinal truth of the narrative in question would be an introduction which combined them both. Here is how John Hutton does it—note how in three arresting sentences we are taken, not only to the crux of the problem at Ephesus, but to the heart of our own predicament to-day: "Wasn't it too bad of those who taught them the rudiments of the Christian faith—to leave those poor innocents in their little boat with nothing but oars! Not telling them that they might step a mast and let loose a sail, for there was always a favouring breath on the face of those waters! What a fool indeed a man would be who should decide to-day to cross the Atlantic, rowing!"

v

If I have dwelt at some length upon this question of how to begin, it is because it is so essential to gain your hearers' interest at the outset. Those first two or three minutes are vitally important. But now we pass to the main body of the sermon. Is the time-honoured usage of divisions—"heads," as they are called—to be recommended? My advice would be to avoid any slavish bondage to tradition at this point. It is certainly not necessary that all sermons, like Gaul, should be divided into three parts. There is no intrinsic sanctity in the tripartite sermon division, nor is it (as some appear to hold) a prerequisite of sound doctrine and essential to salvation. Sometimes your discourse may have six heads, sometimes none. Vary your methods deliberately. Cultivate flexibility. It is bad to cast all your sermons in one mould, so that people know infallibly in advance what shape they will be. Principal Rainy once spoke of sermons to which congregations listened "with respectful resignation, foreseeing clearly how it was all to be, and conscious that mental consuetude had superseded mental life." Refuse to allow any one form of sermon structure to dominate your preaching. In any case, a sermon ought to be a living thing of flesh and blood: do not, therefore, let the bones of the skeleton obtrude themselves unduly. It is the finished building men want to see, not the builder's scaffolding. "The well is deep and you must have something to draw with. But there is no need," says Dr. W. R. Maltby, "to make people drink out of the bucket, still less to chew the rope."

The value of heads is, of course, that they drive home to your hearers' minds the truth for whose acceptance you are pleading. They focus the issue, and so help towards obtaining a verdict. They may stick in the memory when all the rest has been forgotten. Some texts indeed supply their own divisions. Thus, if you are to preach on "The Church at Worship," from the words "They continued stedfastly in the apostles' doctrine and fellowship, and in breaking of bread, and in prayers"; or on "The Fight of Faith," from the apostolic injunction "Watch ye, stand fast in the faith, quit you like men, be strong"; or on "The Four Dimensions of Redeeming Love," from the prayer of intercession "That ye may be able to comprehend with all saints what is the breadth, and length, and depth, and height"—it will hardly be necessary to search far for your divisions, for in each case they are shouting at you from the text itself. With other texts, again, appropriate heads reveal themselves on due consideration and reflection. You are going to preach, let us say, on the words "Looking unto Jesus." What does a steady Christward look involve? It means looking outward, and not inward; upward, and not downward; forward, and not backward. There, then, are your divisions: and you proceed to show that the characteristic trend and direction of our life as Christians must be outward to the objective facts of revealed religion (though of course you will express this differently), not inward to our subjective moods and processes; upward to our divine destiny, "the measure of the stature of the fulness of Christ," not downward to any earthy origins; forward to the greater disclosures Christ has yet to make to us, not backward to the record of past attainment. Or suppose that one day, feeling constrained—as you often will—to lead your people to the very crux of God's dealings with them, you take the texts from Hebrews: "It was not possible that the blood of bulls and of goats should take away sins"; "He hath appeared, to put away sin by the sacrifice of Himself." Your theme is man's desperate dilemma and God's decisive answer. You begin by remarking that the whole history of humanity has been the record of the age-long endeavour to answer the stubborn question, How to make peace with life, How to be right with God. You proceed to point to three classic answers to the problem, three historic expedients which have been tried: the answer of the Jew, the answer of the Greek, the answer of the Roman. You show that each of us has in his constitution something of all three: something of the Jew, who hoped to deal with sin by the intricacies of a religious cult; something of the Greek, who thought to deliver his soul aesthetically and intellectually; something of the Roman, who trusted to moralism and disciplined conduct. Finally, where all three answers break down, through the night of man's despair comes God's answer, smiting the darkness like a sudden dawn. Every other experiment fails: only Christ's—the experiment of the Cross—triumphantly succeeds.

> All for sin could not atone:
> Thou must save, and Thou alone.

It was quite a common practice with preachers of a former generation to announce the main divisions of their subject at the very outset of a sermon. Now this is bad psychology. It gives everything away. It holds no surprises in reserve. It may, indeed, if used on rare occasions prove effective enough. But, on the whole, it is apt to be destructive of interest if people know in advance exactly where you intend to lead them. You handicap yourself if you divulge incontinently the heads you are proposing to use. But let me repeat, whether you formally announce any divisions or not, you must have them clear in your own mind. It is quite fatal to embark on a sermon without having a plainly charted course to follow. How can you hope to have any freedom or conviction in delivery if there is no connecting-thread running through from start to finish, no measured march and progression of thought? Far too many sermons wander erratically from one thing to another, going off at sudden tangents, perpetrating aimless involutions, anon returning upon their own tracks, moving in circles, with divisions overlapping, heads leading to anticlimax, transitions muddy and blurred. The manuscript of Carlyle's essay on Robert Burns went for revision before publication to Jeffrey of the *Edinburgh Review*. When the proof sheets came, the author found—he complained—"the first part cut all into shreds—the body of a quadruped with the head of a bird, a man shortened by cutting out his thighs and fixing the knee-caps on the hips"; and Carlyle refused to let his work appear "in such a horrid shape." His words might stand as a description of a certain class of sermon—misshapen, disjointed, lop-sided and ill-proportioned. Make sure that each point you are going to include receives due weight. Avoid giving so much space to the earlier and perhaps subordinate stages of your argument that you have to foreshorten and telescope the matters of main importance. Aim at a cumulative effect. Keep your most telling points to the last. Lord Palmerston, whose style was apt sometimes to be slipshod and untidy, was speaking one day in Parliament. "I think," he declared, "the honourable member's proposals an outrageous violation of constitutional propriety, a daring departure from traditional policy, and, in short, a great mistake." Bathos, which can play havoc with a sentence, can also damage seriously the total structure of a sermon. Never forget you are working for a verdict. You are hoping and praying to leave your people face to face with God in Christ. That goal must never fade from sight. Make the whole sermon an ascent thither. Construct it with that end in view. Fashion it with that deliberate design; and please God, it will lead men through the outer and the inner courts to the altar of incense, and the Holy Place, and the very presence of the Lord.

VI

This brings us to the crucial matter of sermon-endings. There are preachers who experience the greatest difficulty in drawing to a conclusion. "I must desist," exclaims Beecher, taking a sudden grip of himself at the close of his great discourse on "Hindrances to Religious Life," and openly and undisguisedly ramming on the brakes, "I must desist! The clock gets through before I do, every Sunday. I would that it were slower; for, though I often begin sorrowfully and heavily, the time for me to stop never arrives that I do not feel that I would fain continue till the going down of the sun." No doubt, with a Beecher in the pulpit, men may listen gladly for hours on end. But if you are wise, you will cultivate conciseness. And it is no easy art. Someone once asked Woodrow Wilson how long he took to prepare a ten-minute speech. "Two weeks," was the answer. "How long for a speech lasting an hour?" continued the questioner. "One week," declared the President. "How long for a two-hour speech?" "I am ready now!" Prolixity needs no midnight oil; but to be concise, to achieve compression, to nail down the issue and bring the whole matter to a terse and trenchant close—*hoc opus, hic labor est.* But such toil and care are never wasted. You desire your sermon, under God, to make a difference to human lives. You hope that the result may be some vow secretly ratified, some bondage broken, some cross more resolutely shouldered, some song in the night more bravely sung, some area of life more thoroughly surrendered to the sovereignty of Christ. The weakness of too many sermons is that they meander along and beat about the bush; never bringing the hearer to the point of saying, "This means me"; never leaving him facing Christ and asking, "Lord, what wilt Thou have me to do?" They are like the Abana river, making a brave show for part of its course, but losing itself eventually and dying out and vanishing in the waste. See to it that your sermon shall not hirple vaguely to a lame, ineffectual close. Why should the Word of the Lord peter out in the desert sands? Clinch your message as decisively as you can, and do not hesitate to use the note of direct personal appeal.

In thus urging upon you the crucial importance of your final paragraphs and sentences, I am not suggesting the use of elaborate perorations. Far from it. The day of the florid, self-conscious climax is past. People are rightly suspicious of, and tend to grow restive under, a sermon culminating in a blaze of literary fireworks, like a sonata with a noisy coda. *Diminuendo*, not *crescendo*, ought to be the rule as you draw near the end. Much better conclude quietly and even abruptly than indulge in any declamatory pyrotechnics. If you wish to see how powerful and effective the abrupt close can be, read some of Reinhold Niebuhr's sermons. You will never weaken the force of your final appeal by keeping it restrained. In nine cases out of ten, quiet notes are better there than crashing chords. No doubt there are exceptions. One occasion in St. George's, Edinburgh, was long spoken of with bated breath by those who were present. It was a Communion Sunday, and Dr. Alexander Whyte had chosen his text from the story of Gethsemane. He took his hearers into the darkness of the Garden, and spoke of our Lord's prayers, of the anguish of the conflict and the sweat of blood; he spoke of the seamless robe with the red marks of that agony upon it; then suddenly he broke off into Mark Antony's appeal to the citizens of Rome:

> If you have tears, prepare to shed them now.
> You all do know this mantle: I remember
> The first time ever Caesar put it on;
> 'Twas on a summer's evening, in his tent—

and the preacher, having quoted the almost unbearably moving passage, added the cry that broke from the Roman's lips when the crowd at last caught fire— "Now let it work." Then back to the Garden, and the place of prayer, and the dark betrayal night, and the eternal love that agonized for sin; and it is said that when the sermon closed that day with a great shout "Now let it work!" the spiritual effect was well-nigh overwhelming.

Such occasions, however, are the exceptions which prove the rule. Have you noticed how often there comes in the greatest literature, after the surge and passion of a mighty theme, the contrasted beauty of a quiet and measured close? You have it in the Greek tragedians : if Aeschylus and Sophocles sometimes bring the dramatic tension near to breaking-point, they invariably relax it in the final scene. You have it in the closing lines of *Paradise Lost*, of the *Idylls of the King*, of the *Tale of Two Cities*, of *Sohrab and Rustum*, of *The Everlasting Mercy.* Inexpressibly moving is the long falling close of Matthew Arnold's poem, in which —after the noise and dust of conflict, and the desolating grief of the father who unwittingly has slain his son—we are made to see the majestic river Oxus flowing on

> Out of the mist and hum of that low land,
> Into the frosty starlight. . . .
> A foil'd circuitous wanderer:—till at last
> The long'd-for dash of waves is heard, and wide
> His luminous home of waters opens, bright
> And tranquil, from whose floor the new-bath'd stars
> Emerge, and shine upon the Aral Sea.

You have it superbly in the twenty-ninth Psalm, where whirlwind and tempest and thunder give way in the last verse to a still small voice: "The Lord will give strength unto His people; the Lord will bless His people with peace." You have it at the end of St. Paul's magnificent description to the Corinthians of death and the hereafter, of crashing worlds and tempest blasts, of judgment and the resurrection : suddenly comes the subduing hush—"Therefore, my beloved brethren, be ye stedfast, unmoveable, always abounding in the work of the Lord, forasmuch as ye know that your labour is not in vain in the Lord."

Let these things be your pattern. Men are not saved by declamation, nor are souls carried on the wings of peroration into the Kingdom of Heaven. Cultivate the quiet close. Let your last words of appeal have in them something of the hush that falls when Christ Himself draws near. Remember that, even at the best, "we prophesy in part," and that "whether there be tongues, they shall cease." But if, when our poor stammering words have fallen silent, there comes forth then out of the silence the one eternal Word; if men are able in that silence to hear even though only dimly and far away the challenging and healing cadences of the voice of God, the work will have been done, and we shall not have preached in vain.

CHAPTER IV

THE PREACHER'S TECHNIQUE

" What skill doth every part of our work require, and of how
much moment is every part ! To preach a sermon, I think, is not
the hardest part ; and yet what skill is necessary to make plain
the truth, to convince the hearers ; to let in the irresistible light
into their consciences, and to keep it there, and drive all home ;
to screw the truth into their minds, and work Christ into their
affections ; to meet every objection that gainsays, and clearly to
resolve it ; to drive sinners to a stand, and make them see there is
no hope, but they must unavoidably be converted or condemned :
and to do all this so for language and manner as beseems our work,
and yet as is most suitable to the capacities of our hearers. This,
and a great deal more that should be done in every sermon, should
surely be done with a great deal of holy skill. So great a God,
whose message we deliver, should be honoured by our delivery
of it."—RICHARD BAXTER.

I

THERE was a day when that flaming prophet of
the eighteenth century, George Whitefield, was
preaching to a vast throng on the power of saving faith.
The pride of reason and worldly wisdom, he declared,
would lead the soul downward to inevitable destruc-
tion: only faith in Christ led heavenward. To drive
the point home to his hearers' minds, he used an
illustration. He begged them to imagine a blind man,
with a dog, walking on the brink of a precipice. So
vividly did the preacher describe the scene, so acute
became the tension as he brought the blind man
nearer and nearer to the fatal edge, that suddenly Lord

Chesterfield, who was sitting in the congregation, sprang up exclaiming, "Good God! The man's gone!" "No, my lord," answered Whitefield, "he is not quite gone; let us hope that he may yet be saved." Then he went on to preach deliverance from the delusions of blind self-trust through faith in Jesus Christ.

Now, we may not possess one-tenth of George Whitefield's dramatic imagination. Nevertheless, the art of illustration is a thing no preacher can afford to neglect. Abstract truth has to be translated into concrete terms, if it is to impinge upon the average mind. The preacher who will not condescend thus to translate his meaning, who disdains the use of illustration, considering it undignified and puerile, is being very foolish. Surely our Lord's example is decisive here. Jesus did not speak of the efficacy of importunate prayer: He showed us a man shamelessly hammering at his neighbour's door at midnight. He did not say that wrong personal relationships were inimical to religious reality: He said it would be wise to leave our gift before the altar, and go and make peace with our brother, and then come back and offer the gift. When a certain jurist, an expert in definitions, demanded "Who is my neighbour?" the answer was "A certain man went down to Jericho," and the story of the Good Samaritan. Truth made concrete will find a way past many a door where abstractions knock in vain.

This is an art, of course, which calls for careful handling. Illustrations dragged in at random and needlessly multiplied betoken a slovenly mind. Any illustration which is only doubtfully relevant to the main theme ought to be rigorously banned. No matter how vivid it may be in itself, if it does not immediately light up the particular truth under discussion, exclude it ruthlessly. Otherwise it will simply distract attention and defeat your purpose. On the other hand, illustrations sparingly and appropriately used can be a vital source of power and illumination. You are describing, let us say, man's search for God, the soul's age-long quest for spiritual reality, and the thrilling moment of supreme discovery. Have you read Madame Curie's Life? Do you remember the moving account of the night of magic when, after years of experimenting, she saw across the darkness of the unlit laboratory the first faint streak of phosphorescent blue, and knew that it was radium? Or suppose you are speaking of the remorse which lashes the guilty soul in the hour of its awakening. There is an unforgettable instance you might adduce—the dramatic moment in *Saint Joan* where the Chaplain, who has stood and watched the end, consenting to the death of the saint, bursts in suddenly upon the Earl of Warwick with the lamentable cry, "I let them do it. If I had known I would have torn her from their hands. O God, take away this sight from me! O Christ, deliver me from this fire that is consuming me! She cried to Thee in the midst of it: Jesus! Jesus! Jesus! She is in Thy bosom; and I am in hell for evermore." Or, once again, your theme may be the companionship of Jesus: you are trying to show the power of that companionship to keep life calm and strong and undefeated through days of stress and storm. You recall how Joseph Conrad, in *The Mirror of the Sea*, quotes from a letter of Sir Robert Stopford, who commanded one of the ships with which Nelson chased to the West Indies an enemy fleet nearly double in number. Describing the desperate hardships of that daring adventure, Stopford wrote: "We are half-starved, and otherwise inconvenienced by being so long out of port. But our reward is—we are with Nelson!" How much deeper and more ineffable the serenity of those who through all the hazards and uncertainties of life can say, "We are with Christ!"

The question may well be raised, How is the preacher to obtain an adequate store of illustrative material? I would warn you against being content to allow others to do this garnering for you. Ready-made collections of illustrations are a snare. Omnibus volumes of sermon anecdotes are the last refuge of a bankrupt intelligence. The best illustrations are those which come to you as the harvest of your own reading and observation. In this realm as in others, there is far more zest and thrill in personal discovery than in second - hand borrowing. Be your own anthologist. Little incidents of daily life, significant happenings in the world around you, moving pages in the books you read—all can serve to illuminate the truth committed to your charge. These things are apt to be fugitive and memory precarious: therefore note them down. Elaborate card-indexing of illustrations is a work of supererogation. If a passion for mental tidiness leads you to adopt it, well and good: only beware lest the mechanism of cross-references and the like becomes despotic! For those of us to whom such intricate and even formidable methods must remain counsels of perfection, quite beyond the compass of our less disciplined ways, something much simpler—a loose-leaf commonplace book, with headings—will prove adequate. It scarcely matters how rough-and-ready such a compendium may be, as long as it is veritably your own, sheaves of your own harvesting from the fields of literature and of life. In any case, avoid over-loading. Do not scorn the aid of illustration, but use it sparingly in your sermons, and with discretion. And remember the maxim : Better one illustration that is strong and apt and gripping than ten that are shoddy and irrelevant and sentimental.

II

Passing on to the place of quotations in preaching, we should do well to reaffirm the same rule: be sparing. "Let your moderation be known unto all men." People are not really so avid as some preachers suppose to learn what Confucius said in 500 B.C., or Emerson in A.D. 1850, or the Brains Trust in 1945. Beyond a certain point, the formula "As So-and-so has said" tends to become for some hearers merely irritating, for others positively soporific. Reference was made in an earlier lecture to St. Paul's sermon at Athens, its points of strength and of weakness. It is not without significance that the occasion when the apostle, oppressed perhaps by the shadow of Demosthenes, appears to have argued with himself, "If they want literary allusion—poetry, philosophy, comparative religion—let them have it," was one of the conspicuously less successful days of his ministry: so that going on from there to Corinth, and meditating as he journeyed on the recent disappointment, he "determined not to know anything save Jesus Christ, and Him crucified."

There is one class of quotations which might well be dispensed with altogether—those which have grown hackneyed and threadbare through over-use. It would be much kinder to W. E. Henley and A. H. Clough if all preachers everywhere would agree to give "Invictus" and "Say not, the struggle nought availeth" a complete rest for the next ten years. It is a different matter, of course, when some commonplace allusion can be set in a suddenly new light or viewed from an unfamiliar angle. Take, for example, Sir Oliver Lodge's dictum, "The modern man is not worrying about his sins." I wonder in how many thousand sermons that remark has made a punctual reappearance? Ought it not now to be disqualified, and to have its sermon-licence suspended *sine die*? Certainly, if only the obvious sense of the words is intended. But suppose that one day in a sermon you are concerned to emphasize the crucial paradox, so imperfectly understood by many, that the more a man sins the less he is able to realize that he is a sinner (the damaging thing about sin being what the Bible calls its unconscious "hardening," its ominous way of blinding a man to its own nature and doping his spiritual perceptions without his knowing that anything of the kind is happening): then indeed you may use the familiar quotation with fresh point and force. For now you are setting it in a new light. "Not worrying about his sins"? No, precisely; for sin's characteristic action is to insensitize the soul, to incapacitate it progressively from seeing that there is anything to worry about. Or take, for another example, the stanza from Omar Khayyam:

> Ah Love! could thou and I with Fate conspire
> To grasp this sorry Scheme of Things entire,
>   Would not we shatter it to bits—and then
> Re-mould it nearer to the Heart's Desire!

Banal enough in all conscience, if you are using it merely to illustrate the intractability of life or the disillusionment of a pagan ethic. But there is an inspired flash in Professor A. E. Taylor's comment on the lines when he bids us "put the heart itself at the very head of the list of things to be shattered and remade." There the hackneyed stanza of the Eastern rhymester is suddenly redeemed from its banality, and thrust dramatically into the service of the truth.

Profuse and indiscriminate quotation, then, is a mark of bad preaching. On the other hand, to be able to focus the message at the right moment by quoting some memorable and gripping phrase is a real source of strength. You are preaching, let us say, on the words of the twenty-third Psalm, "He restoreth my soul": God's secret ministry in days of spiritual reaction and fatigue. There comes to your mind a sentence from one of Baron von Hügel's letters: "Am doing what I can for her: pray for her. Have explained how she requires a second conversion—this time against the dust and drear when the physical enthusiasm dwindles." Does that not nail down the issue? Or you are speaking of our Lord's vivid use of the "how much more" argument: "If ye know how to give good gifts unto your children, how much more your Father in heaven!" If parents will sacrifice themselves for their little ones, how much more God! If a man will lay down his life for his friends, how much more God! If you will suffer for one whom you love, how much more God! Do you remember how Lacordaire once dramatized this very truth? "If you would wish to know how the Almighty feels towards us, listen to the beating of your own heart *and add to it infinity*." (Incidentally, there you have the whole book of the prophet Hosea—the man's personal history and his religious message to the world—in one golden sentence.) Or, again, you are dealing with what theologians barbarously describe as "the Kenotic Theory of the Incarnation"—what you will prefer, in your sermon title, to call more simply "The Humility of the Divine": "He divested Himself of the glories of heaven," wrote Paul to the Philippians, "and became a servant and stooped to die upon the Cross." In one of her stories, Sheila Kaye-Smith depicts a character upon whom, as he knelt one day within a church, this great, subduing truth broke with all the force of a personal revelation. "There was not one pang of his lonely, wandering life, no throb or ache or groan of his up to that moment when the light of his eyes and the desire of his heart were taken from him at a stroke, that had not been shared by God. For if man has known the stars, so God has known the dust." There is a sentence which positively demands quotation. And is it not possible that, long after everything else in your sermon has been forgotten, such a shining word as that—"If man has known the stars, so God has known the dust"—may grip the memory of some who heard it, and go to work in secret ways within their hearts?

III

It may be well at this point to say something on the question of language. Two pitfalls against which I have already warned you are professionalism of vocabulary or pulpit jargon, and the temptations of the purple passage: on these nothing further need be said. Let me rather go on to stress one great positive rule which ought to determine your choice of language throughout: Be simple and direct. "People think," exclaimed Matthew Arnold, "that I can teach them style. What stuff it all is! Have something to say, and say it as clearly as you can. That is the only secret of style." Surely Arnold was right. Every man at Pentecost heard the Gospel, we are told, in his own tongue; and that is the basic condition of effective preaching still. Have something to say, and when you are saying it avoid periphrasis and over-elaboration: say it as clearly as you can. Dr. L. P. Jacks maintains that "two lines of Wordsworth—

> But she is in her grave, and, oh,
> The difference to me!

are a more adequate expression of human grief than all the funeral sermons ever preached." It is simple directness, not literary embellishment, that moves the hearts of men.

Let us hark back, by way of contrast, to St. Paul's Cathedral at Christmastide 1624, and listen to this trumpet-toned, tremendous utterance of John Donne. He is speaking of the Psalmist's word, "I will sing of mercy and judgment." "If some King of the earth," cries Donne, "have so large an extent of Dominion, in North, and South, as that he hath Winter and Summer together in his Dominions, so large an extent East and West, as that he hath day and night together in his Dominions, much more hath God mercy and judgment together; He brought light out of darknesse, not out of a lesser light; He can bring thy Summer out of Winter, though thou have no Spring; though in the wayes of fortune, or understanding, or conscience, thou have been benighted till now, wintred and frosen, clouded and eclipsed, damped and benumbed, smothered and stupified till now, now God comes to thee, not as in the dawning of the day, not as in the bud of the spring, but as the Sun at noon to illustrate all shadowes, as the sheaves in harvest, to fill all penuries, all occasions invite His mercies, and all times are His seasons." That is magnificent—but try modelling your sermon language upon it, and the result is likely to be disastrous. Or take this, from a preacher of a very different kind, Talmage of Brooklyn. He has just quoted the railing cry of the impenitent malefactor at Calvary, "If Thou be the Son of God" —and he goes on, "If? Was there any if about it? Tell me, thou star, that in robe of life didst run to point out His birthplace. Tell me, thou sea, that didst put thy hand over thy lip when He bid thee be still. Tell me, ye dead, who got up to see Him die. Tell me, thou sun in mid-heaven, who for Him didst pull down over thy face the veil of darkness. Tell me, ye lepers, who were cleansed, ye dead, who were raised. Is He the Son of God? Aye, aye!, responds the universe. The flowers breathe it—the stars chime it—the redeemed celebrate it—the angels rise up on their thrones to announce it. And yet on that miserable malefactor's 'if' millions shall be wrecked for all eternity." That, again, is great preaching: and you, too, may have— please God, will often have—those moments when language, winged with the emotion of a mighty theme, soars aloft in genuine eloquence. But artificial eloquence, like sham emotion, is a dreadful thing. Learn to prune your language. Reject every expression that is merely florid and ostentatious. Prefer simple and even homely words to those that are abstract and difficult, direct and pointed speech to involved circuitous sentences. Not that you need be arid and prosaic: but you must be lucid. Do not be like the writers Quiller-Couch describes, "perpetually shuffling around in the fog and cotton-wool of abstract terms." Canon Liddon was writing a letter to a friend one dark Christmas from Amen Court. "London is just now," he wrote, "buried under a dense fog. This is commonly attributed to Dr. Westcott having opened his study-window at Westminster." That, of course, was quite unfair. But clarity is a consummation so devoutly to be wished that you must be ready to sacrifice almost anything to achieve it.

In thus urging upon you the necessity of lucid and simple language, I am certainly not suggesting that the best preaching is that which makes a minimum demand upon the hearers for mental exertion and hard thinking. Simplicity is a very different thing from shallowness; and if it is bad to preach over people's heads, not to preach to their heads at all is worse. I trust that to your dying day you will "preach the simple Gospel," but it is well to remember that there is nothing which so stretches men's mental horizons as God's revelation in Christ. It was a true insight that led the apostle to declare, "The world by wisdom knew not God": but it is a deplorable attitude which would divorce evangelism from the duty of disciplined thought. There is a type of preaching which apparently regards it as more important to generate heat than to supply light: sermons devoid of any element of positive teaching, compounded of anecdotes, appeals and homiletical "gush," an affront to any decent man's intelligence, "full of sound and fury, signifying nothing." Some preachers have the fixed idea that the way to reach the human heart is to by-pass the human understanding. It is emphatically mistaken strategy. *Das Denken ist auch Gottesdienst*; and nothing could be more tedious than the preaching which is all uplift and exhortation with no food to feed the mind. Resolve, then, that your pulpit work shall represent not only your truest fervour but also your best thought. Your congregation deserves it, and will welcome it. But even with the deep and difficult themes that tax the mind—with these, indeed, most of all—the rule applies: Be clear, be direct. Rabbi Duncan was discussing with a friend one day the merits and demerits of a certain essay. "Is it not deep?" his friend inquired admiringly. "No," came the blunt expressive answer, "not deep, but drumlie!"

IV

We proceed now to consider the fundamental question of the choice of texts and subjects. To every preacher this is a matter of constant and absorbing concern. Indeed, at the outset of a man's ministry, the prospect of having to find two fresh themes each week may well daunt the imagination and weigh upon the mind. Let me bring to you at this point a word of reassurance based on personal experience. You will discover with relief and delight, as the weeks and years go on, how punctually and unfailingly the promise is ratified, "The Lord will provide." But there is one condition: unremitting Bible study. I have already urged upon you the vital importance of expository preaching. Here let me add that it is only as we live in the Bible—devotionally, and as students of the sacred Word—that we can hope to find the manna falling regularly for our people's need.

Again and again in your reading of the Bible, phrases, sentences, whole passages will leap out from the page, each of them positively thrusting itself upon you, and clamouring "One day you must preach on me!" This is where your private notebooks come into action. When a text has once gripped you, do not let it escape. Jot it down at the head of a page, and underneath it any thoughts, illustrations, potential sermon divisions it may have brought with it. There is a tragic page in the biography of Hector Berlioz the composer, which tells how one night there came to him quite suddenly an inspiration for a new symphony. The theme of the first movement, an Allegro, was ringing in his head: he knew he ought to capture it there and then, and set the music down in manuscript, but he refrained. The following night it returned, and again he heard the Allegro clearly, and sang it to himself, and even seemed to see it written down: but again he failed to take his pen. The next day, when he awoke, all remembrance of it was gone: the lovely melody refused to be recaptured, and the symphony which might have thrilled the world was never written. Let that sad episode be a warning. No elaborate system of tabulation is necessary. All you require is a single reference at the top of a page, and a couple of lines of comment. Very often as you turn the pages of such a reference-book you will find that your theme has been given you; and in a dry season you will thank God you have a reservoir!

It is hardly necessary perhaps to point out that there is one obligation which the very act of preaching from the Word of God binds upon us. I mean the duty of exegetical honesty. There are some sermons which, starting out from a word of Scripture, proceed quite flagrantly to violate the intention of the original writer. This practice of importing alien meanings into texts is strenuously to be discountenanced. To say this is not, of course, to suggest that allegorizing is necessarily bad; nor does it imply a rigid and excessive literalism distrustful of all spiritual lines of interpretation. There is no reason why you should not, occasionally at least, extend the reference of a text beyond its immediate setting. For example, when Jesus declared "What God hath joined together let not man put asunder," He was speaking specifically of marriage and divorce. But the principle there proclaimed runs through the whole of life; and therefore you might well preach from that text on some of those other God-intended alliances which we break at our peril—Faith and Reason (so tragically divorced in the long conflict between the Church and Science), Evangelism and Ethics, Justice and Mercy, Freedom and Discipline, Man the Sinner and Christ the Saviour. Or again, take the closing words of Psalm cx: "He shall drink of the brook in the way, and go on with lifted head." It would be pedantic to deny your right to use such words for a sermon on some of the soul-refreshing streams—Nature, Art, Friendship, the Lord's Day, the Bible, Prayer—which God has provided along our pilgrim road. But the strongest and most helpful preaching is that which expounds a text or passage in dynamic relationship to its actual setting in Scripture. Loyalty to the Word of God demands scrupulous care in exegesis. Doubtless it would be possible, on the basis of the text "The simplicity that is in Christ," to paint a vivid picture of the homeliness of the Galilean ministry—simple in its lowly origins, simple in speech, in companionship, in teaching, in faith. But we are using Scripture quite illegitimately if we fail to show that what the apostle had in mind was not primarily the simplicity of Jesus at all, but the necessity of simple and single-hearted devotion towards Jesus on the part of Christian converts. Or again, it is more than questionable to use King Agrippa's famous dictum, "Almost thou persuadest me to be a Christian," in the sense that here was a soul openly acknowledging the ultimate dilemma, avowedly trembling on the verge of spiritual decision. In point of fact, it seems to have been stinging disdain that inspired the words (though, of course, the bravado may have been self-defence, a smart retort disguising an uneasy conscience): "At this rate, Paul, you will be thinking you have made a Christian of me!" The point is that it is imperative to allow the Scripture to speak its own message. Build your sermons on a solid foundation of accurate exegesis. Be honest with the Word of God!

Such strict attention to basic meanings carries with it rich rewards. In the very process of tracking down the original sense of a text or passage, you will find new suggestions leaping out upon you. To take just one case in point, there is that lovely affirmation of St. Paul to the Philippians: "The peace of God, which passeth all understanding, shall keep your hearts and minds through Christ Jesus." Even as it stands in the Authorised Version, it is moving and expressive. But notice how much more vivid it becomes when the verb is given its full meaning. "The peace of God shall keep guard over, shall stand as sentry to, your hearts and minds." It will hold the fort in the day of siege, and keep the central citadel inviolate. There, surely, is a conception of inner peace far removed from the sentimentalisms which have all too often blemished this noble theme. Christian serenity, as the apostle envisages it, is no passive exemption or easy immunity from the assaults of life: it is the active strength of a God-garrisoned heart.

In your choice of subjects it is wise, as a general rule, to avoid the bizarre and the sensational. It is easy enough to hit upon quaint, outlandish texts; easy enough, by announcing such a text, to intrigue your congregation with the thought—"Now what in all the world will he be able to make of that?" But there is really very little merit in such performances. The chances are that they will leave an impression of the preacher's ingenuity rather than of the majesty of God: and that is failure devastating and complete. Far better gird yourself to grapple with John iii. 16 or Matthew xi. 28 than spend your time pursuing eccentric texts or fashioning odd and startling sermon-titles. "Remember Peniel," says Dr. W. R. Maltby, "and wrestle with the great themes, even if they throw you."

At the same time, it is worth recognizing the fact that on page after page of the Bible there are texts possessing a quite peculiar quality of grip, a dramatic power of arresting attention from the very moment they are announced. To preach from such a text is to implant in your hearers' minds a seed which may go on germinating long after the sermon itself has been forgotten. What converted Spurgeon was not the Methodist lay preacher's sermon in the chapel at Colchester: it was his text—"Look unto Me and be ye saved, all the ends of the earth." "He had not much to say, thank God," declared Spurgeon afterwards, "for that compelled him to keep on repeating his text, and there was nothing needed—by me, at any rate—except his text." When you preach on such a word of Scripture, you start with an enormous initial gain. For from the very outset the text itself goes actively to work, awakening and challenging, smiting and binding up.

For example, you may be anxious to make vivid to your people's minds the wonderful way in which God comes to us through the fact of friendship, using the human relationship—with its experiences of trust, forgiveness and loyalty—to interpret and make luminous for us the very heart and nature of the eternal. Do you remember Jacob's grateful cry to his brother whom he had wronged, when Esau welcomed him back magnanimously after the long estrangement? "I have seen thy face as though I had seen the face of God." How memorably these moving words express the experience of encountering the divine in the human! Such a text, by its own force of impact and momentum, will break through many barriers and thrust deep into heart and conscience.

Or again, you may wish to stress the fact that the most important thing about any man is his final interpretation of life. What does life mean to him, on a total view of it? What is his ultimate verdict on its significance? Is it a fortuitous succession of events, without rhyme or reason, a sorry tale of injustice and frustration? Or is it a plan of God? You might well invite your congregation to approach this question by way of one of the greatest stories in the world. You might take for your text that simple-looking but immensely deep saying of Joseph in Egypt to the men who had enslaved him: "So now it was not you that sent me hither, but God." Set out from that, and your message will have a double reinforcement. For not only is there the dramatic power of the words themselves: there is also the fact that the whole setting of the text in Genesis sheds light upon your theme.

You will be able to show that God does not will the
baffling evils of the world to-day, any more than He
willed the treacherous conduct of Joseph's brethren;
that, nevertheless, when sin has taken the game into its
unclean hands, God is still master of the situation, using
tragedy creatively and making the wrath of man to
praise Him; and that the divine alchemy which thus
brings good out of evil depends on our willing co-
operation, just as it was by refusing the way of bitterness
and recrimination, and by keeping his spirit even at
the darkest hour alert and sensitive to God, that Joseph
was able to turn his necessity to glorious gain and to
lead captivity captive.

Or it may be your purpose on another occasion to
expose the inadequacy of a merely derivative and
borrowed religion in this day of crisis. There is that
swift retort of Jesus to Pontius Pilate, who had been
vaguely sounding our Lord about His claims to sovereignty: "Sayest thou this thing of thyself, or did others
tell it thee of Me?" How that rapier-like challenge
pierces the pretensions of a second-hand religion! Or
you are eager to impress upon your people the Christian's paramount obligation to be an active witness
among men to the truth and the power of the Gospel.
Do you remember the four lepers at the gate of
Samaria who were the first to discover that the besieg-
ing Syrians had fled? "We do not well," they cried,
"this day is a day of good tidings, and we hold our
peace." Or you are concerned to stress the dangers
of a half-hearted, sentimental religion, the need for a

dogged, stubborn devotion which will be ready to face
the austerity of the divine demand and to pay down the
price of discipleship. Jeremiah, writing of the return
of the exiles, has a magnificent word about that: "They
shall ask the way to Zion with their faces thitherward."
Or you may be wanting to strengthen and encourage
those who may be passing through the difficult and
testing times when faith burns low, and the note of
rapture dies out of the Christian song, and dulness and
dryness possess the soul. There is a gloriously re-
assuring word for such a mood in Paul's letter to the
Romans—Dr. Moffatt has translated it: "God never
goes back upon His call." Or you are impressed with
the necessity of setting clear before your people's eyes
the twofold character of the Christian life, the indis-
soluble connection between personal religion and social
passion, between dwelling in the secret place of the
Most High and going forth on crusade against injustice and oppression and all manner of evils everywhere. You will find it all summed up in the noble
words of the prayer of Asa, king of Judah, on the eve
of a great battle long ago: "O Lord our God, we rest
on Thee, and in Thy name we go against this multitude."

Such words of Scripture, used as texts, are weapons
of immense penetrating power. Even if the sermon
should be utterly incommensurate with its theme, the
Word of the Lord on which it is based will not return
unto Him void. There are texts which in themselves
are like a sudden rending of the veil. One of my own

earliest recollections is of a day when **Dr.** Alexander
Whyte of St. George's, Edinburgh, visiting the church
in which my parents were members, preached his
famous sermon on Micah vii. 18. Everything in the
discourse that day has long since faded from memory,
but still across the years there come the tones in which
the preacher repeated over and again his mighty text:
"Who is a God like unto Thee?" Whatever you do,
never forsake the custom of preaching week by week
from the very words of Scripture. Surely the faithful
preacher, with such soul-piercing weapons in his
armoury, can never ultimately fail!

There are times when two weapons are better than
one; and you may occasionally vary the traditional
method by taking two or more texts together. This—
if used sparingly—can be very effective. Thus, for a
sermon on the spiritual pilgrimage of the human soul
in its apprehension of the fact of Christ, you might
bring together the four brief, dramatic utterances:
"Behold the Man," "Behold the Lamb," "Behold
your King," "Behold your God." For has not that
precisely been the pilgrim's progress of many a soul
in relationship to Jesus Christ—fascinated by His
manliness, moved to the depths by His sacrifice,
surrendering to His sovereignty, confessing His
divinity? Or you may sometimes set two texts side
by side by way of contrast. The wonder of the divine
welcome to sinners will stand out arrestingly if you
link Jephthah's curt demand to the elders of Israel,
"Why are ye come unto me now when ye are in dis-

tress?" with the gracious invitation of our Lord, "Him that cometh unto Me I will in no wise cast out"; or the churlishness of Bethlehem, "There was no room," with the hospitality of the king's feast, "Yet there is room!" Or take the Psalmist's cry, "Oh that I had wings like a dove! for then would I fly away and be at rest," in juxtaposition with the apostolic injunction, "Thou therefore endure hardness, as a good soldier"; and immediately you touch the very nerve of one of the most radical tensions in human experience. Sometimes, too, a single word, occurring suggestively in different contexts, will go to work within your mind, and give you the nucleus of a strong and well-knit sermon. You have been impressed, let us say, by the prevalence of two diametrically opposite attitudes in religion: on the one hand, the attitude of some professing Christians who confidently assume that Christ is of their company, whereas in point of fact they have lost Him utterly; and on the other, the attitude of those seeking souls who feel desolately that He is far beyond their reach, whereas in truth He is standing by their side. Do you remember Joseph and Mary who lost Jesus on the Jerusalem road, "supposing Him to have been in the company," and Mary Magdalene who met Him in the garden and knew Him not, "supposing Him to be the gardener"? There the word common to the two passages gives you your theme, and from it you develop your sermon on "Mistaken Suppositions" —the contrasted errors of those who think Christ present when He is absent, and of those who think

Him absent when He is present. Or again, you may have been struck, in reading the Epistles, by the dramatic use Paul makes of two short, simple words—"But now." Again and again they break out of his argument like the sudden note of a trumpet or the beat of a drum. "By the deeds of the law shall no flesh be justified. *But now* the righteousness of God without the law is revealed." "The end of those things is death. *But now* being made free from sin." "Ye were without God in the world: *but now* ye are made nigh." "If in this life only we have hope in Christ, we are of all men most miserable. *But now* is Christ risen from the dead." By the coming of Christ, Paul is saying in these four passages, something has got a foothold in history which turns man's struggle into victory, his sin into redemption, his solitude into divine communion, his setting sun into the daybreak of an eternal morning. And all the way through, that trumpet-toned text will keep sounding forth the truth that God's new era for the sons of men is not mere vision and prophecy, for in Christ it has already appeared. It is not a pious dream, it is historic fact. It is not to-morrow, it is to-day. It is not yonder, it is here. *But now!*

Here let me add that your very calling as expositors of God's Word implies that often you will preach, not from isolated texts or groups of texts, but from whole passages and narratives and incidents. No sermons are more likely to meet with a response of genuine interest and gratitude than those in which the spiritual message of a dozen or a score of verses is faithfully and concisely set forth. A single phrase from Psalm cxxxix or Ephesians i might well provide material for a sermon: but why should you not also make the experiment of taking such a psalm or chapter entire, and grappling with it until you can discern, running right through it from start to finish, one clear line along which to lead your people's thoughts? You will find it a fascinating and rewarding study. Read Isaiah vi analytically, and you may feel an urge to preach on the wings of the seraphim, or the smoke that filled the house: nor is there any reason why you should not obey that urge. Read it as a unity, and there will emerge, clear-cut and decisive, the outlines of a totally different kind of sermon: now, with the whole chapter as your text, you will preach on the three visions which came in rapid succession to the prophet and enter still into the experience of every true servant of the Lord—the vision of God, the vision of himself, and the vision of a waiting world. The point is: do not be in bondage to the tradition of the single text and the isolated phrase. Use the microscope by all means; but do not neglect the wider view and the far horizon. I would even, greatly daring, suggest that you should try occasionally, as a useful discipline of your own mental processes and spiritual perception, to concentrate into one sermon the basic message of a whole book, such as Amos, Hosea, or Revelation. There are tens of thousands of people to-day who are quite unable, where the Bible is concerned, to see the wood for the trees.

You will be doing no small service if, leading them to vantage-points above the lower levels, you show them the country spread out before them like a map, and the glory of the land of far-stretching distances.

Further, I would advise you in the choice of texts and subjects to aim at comprehensiveness. Your task is to surprise your hearers with "the many-coloured wisdom of God," not to bore them with the restricted aspect of the truth which happens to appeal most to yourself. It is a wearisome business for a congregation when the man in the pulpit incessantly thrusts his own preferences, insights and viewpoints upon them, as though these were the sum total of the evangel. Of course, the personal equation is bound to influence your work: and that message alone will ring true which a man can call "my Gospel." But that is no reason why you should jog monotonously down the well-beaten tracks, or drag your people week by week along the grooves of your own favourite ideas. Take stock of your pulpit work from time to time. Ask yourself: "Is there some aspect of the faith which I have been neglecting? Some doctrine which has been missing from my teaching? Have I been doing justice to the many-sided message of the Scriptures?" Use the diversity of the Word of God to widen your own spiritual range. Reject resolutely the tempting tyranny of the obvious and the congenial. And remember Paul's parting words to the elders of Ephesus: "I have not shunned to declare unto you the whole counsel of God."

V

This brings another important matter into view—
the value of "courses" of sermons. Much is to be
said for the tradition of intimating from time to time a
connected sequence of studies on one particular theme
or section of Scripture. For one thing, this method
gives scope for that systematic instruction in Christian
truth which forms so essential a part of any vital
ministry. Moreover, it is an immense gain to the
preacher himself to have his path for the next six or
seven Sundays clearly mapped out in advance. Not
only does it mean a saving of valuable hours which he
might otherwise waste in a haphazard and fruitless
search for texts; there is also the fact that, once the
subject is fixed, his mind keeps working at it sub-
consciously, gathering materials and hammering them
into shape. Spurgeon argued against courses of
sermons on the ground that the Holy Spirit does not
work that way: to prescribe a route in advance by
announcing a list of projected themes is to lay a fetter
upon one's own soul, and to limit the possibilities of
divine inspiration. That is, to say the least of it,
debatable—did not an apostle once describe the Holy
Spirit as the "Spirit of saving discipline" (*sophronismos*)?
—but perhaps there is enough truth in it to serve as a
warning. Just as it is unwise, as a general rule, to give
away your proposed divisions or heads at the outset of
a sermon, so the announcement of a consecutive series
may seem to involve surrendering that invaluable

weapon of the preacher—the element of surprise. On the other hand, it will be found that most congregations will welcome an occasional course of reasonable length: they will feel with relief that there is a satisfactory definiteness in it, as contrasted with the preaching which bandies them about in a desultory fashion from Genesis to Revelation, without plan or system.

"An occasional course"—I emphasize that: for it is inexpedient to stereotype your methods, running one series of sermons after another all the year round without a break. And "of reasonable length"—that is vitally important. You may have only three or four sermons in a course. As a maximum I would suggest eight or nine. Six would be an ample number. Dr. Alexander Whyte once preached for a whole winter in St. George's, Edinburgh, on one text, Luke xi. 1, "Lord, teach us to pray": but then he was a giant of the pulpit, and could dare things not permitted to lesser men. It is told of one of the early eighteenth-century ministers of the City Temple, Robert Bragge, that he announced a course of sermons on the mystical meaning of Joseph's coat of many colours, and continued it Sunday by Sunday for four months. As a contemporary described it:

> Eternal Bragge, in never-ending strains,
> Unfolds the wonders Joseph's coat contains;
> Of every hue describes a different cause,
> And from each patch a solemn mystery draws.

The extraordinary thing is that Bragge's popularity with his congregation appears to have survived even that severe and searching test. But that was two centuries ago, and is not for emulation to-day. Spurgeon confessed that the epistle to the Hebrews came near being ruined for him in his youth by a seemingly interminable series of discourses to which it was his fate to listen. "I wished frequently that the Hebrews had kept the epistle to themselves, for it sadly bored one poor Gentile lad. That epistle exhorts us to *suffer* the word of exhortation, and"—he added grimly—"we did so." The passion for comprehensiveness is doubtless a laudable virtue; but it can ruin a man's preaching unless it is held in check by common sense and by a judicious application of the art of omission.

Take, for example, the book of Jeremiah. Might it not be possible, by careful planning and wise selection, to concentrate the main message of Jeremiah into a course of six or eight addresses? The experiment is at least worth trying. It will certainly involve an immense amount of preliminary study, mental spade-work and spiritual discipline. But granted fidelity of preparation, such a course of sermons is likely to meet with an eager and deeply encouraging response. Let me—taking Jeremiah still as illustration—reinforce my plea for this kind of preaching by urging upon you three considerations. For one thing, the message of the book is so decisively significant for the present hour. Do you wish a vivid interpretation of God's will for a time of national crisis? You will find that here. Are you concerned about the part that organized religion ought to play in face of the challenge of the social and economic conditions which mould the lives of men? You will find that here. Are you anxious to show what faith can say about the mysteries of Providence, and what God means by allowing life sometimes to be so terribly difficult for those who take His way? You will find that here. Moreover, the man himself is such a fascinating study. Jeremiah has laid bare to us, not only the outward events of his life, but also the inner struggles of his spirit. And finally, here is a book which inevitably leads the preacher straight to the burning heart of personal religion. Thus the strength of such a course of sermons is that history and biography become alive, contemporary, challenging; and exposition merges in evangelism.

By way of variety, a series on the message of a book of Scripture might well be followed by a set of character studies. Some preachers are inclined to disdain this type of sermon and to minimize its usefulness. They regard it as merely an easy and not particularly commendable expedient involving a minimum of thought and positive teaching. This is really very foolish and unimaginative. In point of fact, few sermons can be so spiritually searching and incisive as those in which the preacher, singling out some character from the vast portrait-gallery of Scripture, shows us the actual man, striving, struggling, sinning, repenting, with the living God intersecting his experience and invading his soul. John Galsworthy, in *Flowering Wilderness*, makes one of his characters, Adrian Cherwell, exclaim: "It's the sudden personal emergency coming out of the blue, with no eyes on you, that's the acid test. Who among us knows how he'll come through it?" What wealth of material lies to your hand in the pages of the Bible, to show how different men react to the sudden personal emergency, leaping on them out of the blue, in the unguarded hour! "Souls at the Crossroads," you might call your sermon sequence: and you speak in turn of Esau, of Balaam, of Samson, of David, of Gehazi, of Daniel—of each man in that crucial hour when, as Browning puts it,

> God stoops o'er his head,
> Satan looks up beneath his feet—both tug.

It will be strange indeed if, through such a course, many in your congregation do not become aware of God dealing with their own souls in judgment and mercy. Or at another time you may plan a series with the title "Encountering Jesus." From the crowded record of the Gospels you choose out six or seven men and women in the moving and dramatic moment when their several paths crossed the path of Jesus—Nicodemus, the woman of Samaria, Zacchaeus, the centurion of Capernaum, the man born blind, the Syrophoenician mother, the dying thief—and it may be that as you endeavour with the aid of imagination (which is just another name for the insight of faith) to reconstruct these scenes, the Gospel story will begin to repeat itself in your congregation; and one here and another there, forgetting all about the preacher and "seeing no man save Jesus only," will register secret decisions and ratify new vows, knowing that to them also it has been given—as veritably and as vividly as to those men and women long ago—to encounter the Saviour of the world.

VI

Let me add, in passing from this question of the choice of texts and subjects, two final remarks. It is possible that, in spite of vigilance and fidelity, bad weeks will occur when inspiration seems to have deserted you: no theme lays a coercive grip upon you, no text cries peremptorily "Preach on me." What are you to do then?

> O for a Muse of fire, that would ascend
> The brightest heaven of invention!—

But waiting for that kindling moment is a risky business, with Sunday rushing on inexorably. Nor is it advisable in days when the going is difficult and the fire burns low to take the easy way out and preach an old sermon over again. Certainly there is no reason, if you have once toiled over a sermon and put your best into it, why you should not use it a second time; and the advice sometimes given, "burn the lot," is surely more reckless than heroic. Thomas Chalmers once had an unusual experience. He was growing weary of the gaping crowds that thronged his ministry; and one Sunday morning, being determined to end this displeasing vogue and to prevent the annoyance of overcrowding, he intimated that in the evening he proposed to preach, not a different sermon, but the same one which he had just delivered. That night the church doors were rushed! But have a care what moral you deduce from that story. You will be wise not to discard your old sermons. But you will be doubly wise never to have recourse to any of them as a means of escape from the heavy self-discipline, mental and spiritual, of unlit days and difficult weeks. "Thou therefore endure hardness, as a good soldier of Jesus Christ."

But is there any positive and practical counsel one can give against such hours of emergency, when the mind seems barren, the supply exhausted, and the harp hangs silent on the willows?

> Biting my truant pen,
>> Beating myself for spite,
> Fool, said my muse to me,
>> Look in thy heart, and write.

That is the first essential. Get closer to God. Ponder anew your own immeasurable debt to Him. Has He not delivered, time and again, your eyes from tears, your feet from falling, your soul from death? That recollection will loosen the grip of the low mood from your spirit, as spring breaks up the grip of winter. Then open your Bible. Do not pursue elusive texts. Stop racking your brain for a subject. Take a whole psalm, a complete Gospel incident, or a solid section from an epistle of St. Paul. Set yourself to interpret it faithfully. I am almost inclined to believe that the Holy Spirit deliberately sends such bad weeks occasionally, in order to force the preacher to rediscover the

virtue of plain, downright exposition. Your wisdom
at such a time is to desist from weaving fancies around
isolated phrases of Scripture: it is to take an entire
passage, and let the Word of God speak for itself. It
may be you will find that it is precisely the sermon
wrought out in these difficult, ebb-tide hours for which
God reserves His richest blessing.

The other remark to be added here is this. Resolve
that every sermon you preach shall be in the truest
sense your own. This indeed is involved in the very
nature of the Gospel itself.

> What we have felt and seen
> With confidence we tell.

"This," wrote Elgar at the end of the original score of
his great oratorio *The Dream of Gerontius*, "this I saw
and knew"; and there is little hope of preaching being
effectual unless the preacher can implicitly say the
same. Every sermon must have something of your
own life-blood in it. It is your personal act of witness.
"That which we have seen with our eyes, and our hands
have handled, of the Word of life, declare we unto you."
Not that you are to bestrew your discourse with frag-
ments of autobiography! Keep the first personal
pronoun severely in the background. The pulpit is
no place for indulging a propensity to egotistical
reminiscence. To say that the preacher's sermon
should be his own does not at all mean the obtruding
of self into the picture. It does emphatically mean that
God has a higher ideal in view for His commissioned

servants than that they should be mere borrowers and copyists.

It is hardly necessary to labour the point that to borrow another man's thoughts, ideas and expressions, and to present them as one's own, may be one way of reducing labour and maintaining the supply, but in God's eyes it is to be a castaway. Here is someone, let us say, who is so preoccupied throughout the week with a medley of good works, all of them doubtless legitimate and worthy in their own way, that at the week-end, finding himself sermonless and in desperate straits, he is driven to use another man's material, "reaping where he has not sown, and gathering where he has not strawed." Is it likely that such preaching should ring true? May not such a habit, if persisted in, neutralize and negative the grace of the preacher's ordination? Must it not imperil his spiritual vitality, and ultimately jeopardize his soul? The five wise virgins who refused to share their surplus oil with their five foolish sisters were not being stingy and cantankerous: they were simply giving realistic expression to the undoubted truth that in this world there can be no shining with a borrowed light. Far better the poorest and most halting discourse that is veritably a man's own than the most elaborate work of art tainted with the breath of plagiarism. But indeed it were superfluous to emphasize this further. The basic note of preaching must ever be reality. And where is honour towards God to be looked for if not in the work of those who are His heralds?

VII

We pass now from the making of the sermon to its delivery. You have found your message. In the quietness of your study you have pondered it and wrestled with it. You have fashioned it to the best of your ability. But that is not the end. There still remains the all-important final stage of the process. You have now to send that message to work as a living thing in other minds. You have to endeavour, face to face with a company of your fellow men and women, to get the Word of the Lord out of your heart into theirs.

No wise man will underrate this ultimate task. Far too many a competent and carefully constructed sermon has been nullified and ruined by a careless or incompetent delivery. To-day, more than ever before in the history of preaching, this matter is vital. Broadcasting has brought right into the homes of the nation distinguished voices speaking on all manner of subjects—literature, politics, science, religion: and people who have thus grown accustomed to well-articulated and effective speech are less likely to be indulgent to a preaching manner that is ponderous or mumbling or uncouth, or to the dull tedium of that hateful thing, the "pulpit voice." The message entrusted to the preacher is not less but far more important than any wireless talk however fascinating on a literary, scientific or sociological theme. That a message of such vast consequence should be delivered in a manner which virtually denies its urgency is witless and inexcusable.

Now here there inevitably arises the question of the relative merits of read and spoken sermons. This is an old debate and it is not necessary to rehearse all the "pros" and "cons." Let me rather make one or two general suggestions on the main issue, and then draw attention to three specific points which have been singularly overlooked.

You will be well advised, whichever method of delivery you are proposing to adopt, to begin by writing out your sermons fully. During the first ten years of your ministry—and perhaps over a much longer period than that—there is no substitute for this essential discipline. It will safeguard your work against diffuseness, ambiguity and redundance. It will make for clarity of thought and perspicuity of style. Therefore establish it as a rule that one of your two sermons each week—some would go further and say both—shall be, not merely drafted, but wrought out in full from beginning to end.

But having your sermon thus completely written, what are you to do with it? Are you to take the manuscript into the pulpit and read it word for word? That this method has manifest advantages is not to be denied. Thus, for example, it ensures that the balanced presentation of a subject, for which the preacher has laboured in his study, shall not be lost. Moreover, it defends a helpless congregation from the worst evils of extemporaneous padding and prolixity! It defends the preacher from the nightmare experience of floundering in the morass, and fumbling in vain for the right word and the telling phrase. Joseph Parker once asked R. W. Dale of Birmingham why he read his sermons; to which Dale frankly replied, "If I spoke extemporaneously I should never sit down." "My command of words," he confessed, "is such that as a young man I could preach standing on my head. To be condensed is my object in writing my sermons." It is eminently desirable that a sermon should be compact, clean-cut and as far as possible free from literary aberrations and logical anacoloutha: herein lies the virtue of the read sermon. Nor ought we to be influenced by what Phillips Brooks once called "the general impression of the piety of extemporaneousness": a crude, erroneous notion, based on a naïve doctrine of the Holy Spirit. Have we not all heard sermons delivered without a scrap of paper which moved us not a whit, and merely left us feeling "The Lord was not in the wind"? And have we not listened to read discourses which were memorable in the deepest sense and charged with spiritual power?

There is, however, another side to this matter. The preacher who suffers himself to be tied slavishly to his manuscript is surrendering something—a quality of directness and pointedness, of versatility and verve and liveliness—which he can ill afford to lose. There is the ever-present danger that the typed or written sermon on the pulpit-desk in front of him may act as a barrier between himself and those to whom he speaks. Christian preaching strikes notes of challenge and appeal

which are almost bound to sound muffled and unnatural where bondage to the written word holds sway.
The minister of the Gospel is essentially a herald of the
most magnificent and moving tidings that ever broke
upon the world; but how shall he make the world feel
the living urgency of the message if he is perpetually
fettered and shackled by the tradition of the read
discourse? If you dispense with your manuscript, and
preach freely from a single page of notes, your sermon
may indeed lose something of artistry and literary
expression; there may be gaps and broken sentences—
occasionally even murdered grammar. "Brethren,"
cried Father Taylor, the sailor-preacher, finding himself entangled in a sentence from whose labyrinthine
subordinate clauses there seemed to be no exit, "I have
lost the nominative of this sentence, and things are
generally mixed up, but I am bound for the Kingdom
anyhow!" You may lose some polished idiom or
nicely rounded phrase; you may perpetrate many an
abrupt and violent anacolouthon. What matter if you
do? Take courage: you are in good company. Are
there no anacolouthistic sentences in the New Testament, beginning one way, ending another? In any
case, what you stand to lose is more than compensated
by the gain in personal grip, in directness and urgency
and reality, in the immediate impact of mind upon
mind and the living encounter of heart with heart.
Do you remember Jeanie Deans, in *The Heart of Mid-
lothian*, telling Reuben Butler of her decision to make
the long journey to London and plead in person for

Effie's life before the king and queen? "Writing winna do it—a letter canna look, and pray, and beg, and beseech, as the human voice can do to the human heart. A letter's like the music that the ladies have for their spinets —naething but black scores, compared to the same tune played or sung. It's word of mouth maun do it, or naething, Reuben." There is something there worth pondering by those whose task it is to plead with men, beseeching them in Christ's stead to be reconciled to God.

It would be very unwise, of course, to prescribe any general rule on this matter. Each man must find his own method for himself. You might decide, for instance, as many preachers have done, to use alternately both methods described, reading one sermon each Sunday and speaking the other. But let me pass on to three facts bearing on this whole debate, which are apt to be strangely overlooked.

First, the preacher's method must be adapted to the needs of the present age. It is no good saying, for example, that because the tradition of read sermons satisfied a former generation it is necessarily valid to-day. It is our lot to have been called to the ministry at a time when the Church is being challenged to get out into the open. All the evidences indicate that this demand will grow even more insistent in the coming years. Can you imagine a preacher facing a crowd in the open-air, the factory, the camp, and reading his address off a manuscript? The thing is absurd. And if your open-air preaching thus delivers you from bondage to the letter, why not carry that immense gain across into your pulpit work in church? Let no man, in this hour when the Church is being challenged to come out from behind its own walls and barriers, reject that opportunity with the disclaimer "It is not in my line." Christ has issued His marching-orders: what else matters? Make up your mind to take a full share of this vital work in the wider field and to meet men on their own ground. Not the least of the results will be a new sense of freedom in your ministry. Having once cast off subservience to your own written words, you will not readily submit to a reimposition of the yoke. Stand fast in the liberty wherewith Christ has made you free!

Second, it is worth emphasizing that freedom of delivery in the pulpit depends upon carefulness of construction in the study. It is surprising how often this point has been missed in the debate between read and spoken sermons. To the question "Ought I to risk oral delivery of my sermon?" the right answer surely is that it all depends on the sermon. Some sermons it would be almost impossible, even for the man who wrote them, to carry in the mind at all. They meander with mazy motion; they return upon their tracks; ideas overlap; single paragraphs trail on and on for pages; there is not one illustration like a beacon to light the way. For such sermons, oral delivery would involve prodigious feats of memory—and that is no true preaching. On the other hand, it should be quite possible for the preacher, without the stiltedness of mechanized memorizing, to get a sure grip and clear conspectus of his own sermon, provided that certain conditions have been observed in the writing of it. These conditions are clarity of logical structure; well-defined divisions and subdivisions; exclusion of ir-relevances; short paragraphs, with a single clear-cut thought in each, not long unbroken stretches, where a dozen ideas jostle; balance and progress and develop-ment; with one or two strong and vivid illustrations marking out the track. The point is that freedom of delivery will tend to vary in direct proportion to accuracy of construction. If you can fashion a sermon which stands out clearly in all its parts before your own mind, the tyranny of the manuscript is broken.

Third, remember that the opening years invariably tend to fix the methods of a man's whole ministry. Any preacher, even the most tongue-tied and diffident, can achieve freedom of utterance—on two conditions: he must be willing to face the necessary self-discipline, and he must begin early enough. Those first years are big with enviable opportunity and critical decision: for it is then that ways and habits are developing which, once formed, are apt to bind irrevocably. In this matter of delivery, every preacher is at the beginning master of his fate. You may be led to adjudge that you can serve God best in your pulpit by reading your sermons. But if you feel another method beckoning you, have no misgivings. Do not precipitately decide against it. If you want to be free, you can.

VIII

As regards pace, I am disposed to propound a mild form of heresy. The orthodox attitude would be to warn you against the errors of a too rapid delivery, and to beg and beseech you to go slow: put on the brake, and keep it on! I suggest that too much *Andante* with never a touch of *Allegro* or even *Presto* can be quite as fatal. You will not, of course, emulate the preacher whom Spurgeon described, "tearing along like a wild horse with a hornet in its ear." Common sense will teach you to regulate speed in accordance with the acoustics of the building in which you are speaking. But just as a dragging organ accompaniment can ruin congregational praise, so a too deliberate pulpit delivery can gravely decelerate interest in the message. Preaching ought to resemble a purposeful, rhythmic march rather than a slow-paced saunter: it is degraded when it becomes a slouch or a shuffle. There are speakers who proceed with such irritating leisureliness that those listening to them can forecast, before each sentence is half-finished, exactly how it is going to end. No congregation ought to be subjected to such a horrid ordeal. If you are temperamentally inclined to dash ahead like an express train, let reasonableness moderate your impetuosity. But if the voice of orthodoxy in these matters has almost persuaded you that *Largo di molto* must be the invariable rule of the pulpit, you would do well to consider whether this tempo—deliberate and stately and dignified, verging sometimes on the ponderous—is really the best adapted for conveying to your hearers' minds a Gospel urgent and glorious and amazing beyond all other tidings in the world.

In tone, no less than in speed, variety is essential. It is strange that so often the effect of standing in a pulpit should be that a man's natural speaking voice is immediately transformed into something forced and artificial and monotonous. Savonarola declared that many a Gospel hearer had "become like unto a rook on a steeple, that, at the first stroke of the church bell, takes the alarm and hath fear, but then, when accustomed to the sound, percheth quietly on the bell, however loudly it be rung." Learn to modulate the voice, and avoid like the plague the conventional pulpit monotone; lest your people, "accustomed to the sound," cease to heed the message. Always begin quietly. Even when your theme, as it develops, takes hold of you irresistibly (as it ought to do if you are truly preaching), bring yourself back again and again deliberately to the conversational level. As Hamlet put it to the players, "In the very torrent, tempest, and, as I may say, the whirlwind of passion, you must acquire and beget a temperance that may give it smoothness." Never bellow! Remember Savonarola's rook perching disdainfully on the bell, "however loudly it be rung." Let yourself go occasionally if the Spirit moves you; but clamour is not necessarily inspiration, and shouting saves no souls. A good sermon can have its total effect reduced fifty per cent by an over-emphatic and hectic delivery; and platitudes which might disclose new meanings if treated quietly become merely tiresome or absurd when shouted and declaimed.

This insistence on being natural applies also to gesture. There is no necessity that the preacher should aim at reproducing the immobility of a graven image; but neither is there any necessity that he should saw the air like a windmill, or behave like a schoolboy with the fidgets. You will be wise, at almost any cost of strenuous self-discipline, to eradicate and eschew all meaningless mannerisms which, so far from adding emphasis to what is being said, serve only to distract. Temperament and individuality play here so large a part that imitation of any kind is bound to be disastrous: the gesture which in one man is right and unexceptionable might be ludicrous in another. Dr. Carnegie Simpson, in his *Recollections*, has described how once as a youth he heard Spurgeon preaching in the old Metropolitan Tabernacle, on the subject of the inspiration of Holy Scripture. At one point the preacher took up some book into his hands, and crying dramatically, "Here is a work of current science—its day will pass," let the volume drop. "Here," he went on, taking up another book, "is a fashionable novel—it soon will be dead," and it also he let fall. Then, taking the big pulpit Bible bodily off its desk, clutching it in his arms and holding it aloft, he cried, "Here is the Word of God which endureth for ever." Spurgeon could dare the startling gesture, and it would be magnificently impressive: but with ninety-nine men out of a hundred the risk of an abrupt descent from the sublime to the ridiculous would be prohibitive. It is a wise rule to be sparing of gesture, and to suffer no movement which is not the natural and instinctive expression of a deeply felt mood.

The fact is that this whole matter of delivery can be resolved into two precepts which are not so paradoxical as they appear: Be yourself—Forget yourself. God has given to each man his own individuality, and standardization is emphatically no part of the divine intention for your ministry. How intolerably dull it would be if every preacher had to be cut to the same pattern! You are to give free rein to your personality. "We are too formal," cried Dr. Alexander Whyte. "We have too much starch in our souls." And he went on, in his downright way: "Starch is more deadly than sin. Your soul may be saved from sin, but scarcely from starch." Henry Ward Beecher was no less outspoken: "There may be a propriety in a man's preaching that will damn half his congregation, or there may occasionally be almost an impropriety that will hurt nobody, and accompanied with the right manner will save multitudes." Do not think that personal idiosyncrasies are merely to be suppressed and levelled out. Be yourself. And do not complain if you cannot be someone else. Nothing is more preposterous or pathetic than the sedulous attempts which are sometimes made to imitate external mannerisms or ways of speech. "David played before the

Lord," says the sacred writer, "on all manner of instruments." If God has made you a clarinet or a flute, do not complain that you are not a violin or a harp. Shall the trumpet say to the oboe, "I have no need of thee"? Or the drum to the 'cello, "I have no need of thee"? Shall the great Master Musician, who controls them all, say to the humblest of His instruments, "I have no need of thee"?

Be yourself, then; but also, forget yourself. You are to use for the delivery of the Word every faculty God has given you; and simultaneously you are to renounce yourself utterly, so that in the end the messenger shall be nothing, the message everything. You are not to cramp or stifle your individuality; but you are to offer it so completely to God upon the altar that, when the service closes, the dominating thought in the worshippers' minds will be, not of any obtrusive human proficiency or cleverness, but only this—"The Lord was in His holy temple to-day!"

We are desperately self-conscious creatures, and that miserable fact of self-love tends to thrust its way into the picture, even in our work for Christ. To achieve release and self-obliteration, one thing is essential for the preacher: as he leads the worship of his congregation, let him see to it that he is worshipping along with them. As he uplifts the supplications of his people to the throne, let him be bowing there himself in heart and mind. Then, when he stands up to preach, he will have found deliverance through worship from the tyranny of self. Not only so, but his words will now come forth throbbing with a fervour and reality totally unlike the pseudo-animation of a pretentious and self-conscious delivery. "When the work of the composer," wrote Jebb of the Greek poets, "failed to be vital and sincere, this, the unpardonable fault, was described by the expressive word *psychros*, frigid. The composition was then no longer a living thing, which spoke to the hearers and elicited a response. It was stricken with the chill of death." Jebb might have been writing there of the Christian preacher. In the moment when sincerity goes, the whole business of preaching is stricken with the chill of death; and the obtrusion of self is always destructive of sincerity. In the last resort, everything depends on the degree in which awareness of self is swallowed up in the vision of God. As he delivers his sermon, the man who has himself entered through worship into the holy place will preach with something of the glow and freedom which mark true inspiration. Among those listening to him there will be some who, as the sermon proceeds, are conscious less of the actual speaker than of a ringing and authentic "Thus saith the Lord!"—some who beyond the human tones will hear, pleading and commanding, the very voice of Jesus. And long after the sermon is finished, that voice will keep sounding on. Paul plants, Apollos waters; but the real issues are wrought out at levels where Paul, Apollos and every other human factor have vanished out of sight. It is not your personality that has to be impressed redeemingly upon other souls—thank heaven for that; it is not you who are to dazzle men with your grasp of the truth, or your powers as a defender of the faith; it is not you who are going to convert souls and unlock the shining gates to which only Jesus has the key. Bring everything you have and are to your ministry—your best craftsmanship, your most concentrated study, your truest technique, your uttermost of self-consecration, your toil and sweat of brain and heart—bring it all without reserve. But when you have brought it, something else remains: *Stand back, and see the salvation of God.*

Chapter V

THE PREACHER'S INNER LIFE

" The zeal for God that is not according to knowledge is a zeal
that dies in the middle years by the pessimism of experience ; but
the zeal that is fed by His broken Body and His outpoured Blood
devours us still, in an age of weariness and cynicism."

BERNARD MANNING.

THERE is a Franciscan story which tells how the
saint on one occasion invited a young novice to
accompany him on a preaching expedition through the
town, and how they passed through one street after
another and eventually returned to their starting-point,
and not a word had been spoken. "But, father," said
the probationer, puzzled and disappointed, "I thought
we were going to preach?" "We have preached," replied Francis, "we were observed as we walked. They
marked us as we went. It was thus we preached."

You have chosen a vocation—or rather, Christ has
chosen you for it—which more than any other calling
in the world depends upon the quality of life and the
total witness of character which by the grace of God a
man may bring to it. "Preaching," inquires Bishop
Quayle, "is the art of making a sermon and delivering
it?"—and he answers his own question: "Why, no,
that is not preaching. Preaching is the art of making
a preacher and delivering that. It is no trouble to
preach, but a vast trouble to construct a preacher."

190

When Gehazi went at Elisha's command to resurrect the dead, he took the prophet's staff with him, but no miracle happened; for the virtue of the staff was negatived by the hands that held it. "I was confirmed," wrote John Milton, "in the opinion that he who would not be frustrate of his hope to write well in laudable things ought himself to be a true poem." Homiletics may indeed be taught by books and lectures; but at the heart of everything stands the personal equation, and the real work is done, not on the level where a man acquires a knowledge of technique and rules and devices, but on the deep levels of self-commitment where he rigorously disciplines his life for love of Jesus Christ. One hesitates to say anything on a matter so intimate and sacred: here words can be but few and faltering. Yet it would be a poor service to analyse the elements of preaching and be dumb about what matters most. "Anything destined to be strong and efficacious in *action*," Father Martindale reminds us, "needs a drastic preparation of *character*." And if there is truth in the saying *pectus facit theologum*, it is no less true that the inner life makes the preacher.

Sometimes it will happen that your most carefully prepared sermon discomfits you by missing fire completely—a salutary if humbling experience. Then is the time to put some searching questions to your own soul: "Why did it fail so palpably? Was it because I had neglected the flame on my own altar? Can it have been that I was so busy preparing my sermon that I omitted to prepare myself?'' Now, just as this discipline of self-preparation is necessary for every sermon a man preaches, so it must form the constant background of his total ministry. I am not suggesting a double standard of sanctification——one level of holiness for the Christian layman as he goes about his business and another for the ordained minister of the Word: for with God there is no respect of persons, and every Christian without distinction is committed to live for Christ with every atom of his being. But I am saying that if I presume to point out to others the heavenward way, while failing to bend all my spiritual energies to its pursuit, I shall receive from God the greater condemnation. The ambassador of Christ shares all men's involvement in sinful corruption, and it was the greatest ambassador who ever lived who confessed himself to be the chief of sinners. But the preacher is essentially a seer, bringing back to men first-hand reports of divine truth and authentic visions of that Jerusalem which is the mother of us all: and if he cannot induce the vision nor evoke it at will, he can at least keep clean the window through which his vision is likely to come. ''Take heed unto yourselves, and to all the flock'' was Paul's parting injunction at Miletus to the elders of the Church——to yourselves first, for only so can the hungry sheep be fed. You must believe intensely and with total conviction, if you are to persuade others to believe. Your own spirit must be subjected to the full force and challenge of Christ's ethic, must be energized, supernaturalized, if you are to bring God's help to bear upon the gaping needs of men. The trouble is, as Richard Baxter put it bluntly to the clergy of his day, that "many a tailor goes in rags, that maketh costly clothes for others; and many a cook scarcely licks his fingers, when he hath dressed for others the most costly dishes." It is a solemnizing thought for any preacher that what he speaks to men in the name of God is going to be mightily reinforced or mercilessly negatived by the quality of life behind it. Chaucer summed it up succinctly when he wrote of his good priest:

> Christes lore, and His apostles twelve,
> He taught, and first he folwed it him-selve.

It might indeed be supposed that the very nature of the preacher's calling would guarantee an invincible fidelity and consecration. But all sacred things are double-edged; and if the tasks of the ministry may be a safeguard and a panoply they have also their peculiar perils, and they exact vengeance from those who handle them with undue familiarity. Robertson of Brighton was right when he spoke of "the hardening influence of spiritual things"; for the prophetic awe and wonder in presence of the revelation of God can all too easily deteriorate into a mere mechanical trafficking with the ordinances of religion. To quote Baxter again: "It is a sad thing that so many of us preach our hearers asleep; but it is sadder still if we have studied and preached ourselves asleep, and have talked so long against hardness of heart, till our own grow hardened under the noise of our own reproofs." There is no sure

defence against that grim and tragic loss of reality and
zeal and faith except in a daily renewed surrender of
life to Christ, nor is there any easy alternative by which
to evade the cost of this rigorous and surgical self-
discipline and commitment.   There is no by-pass road
round Calvary.   "He is like a refiner's fire, and He
shall purify the sons of Levi."

Let us inquire, then, what manner of man the
preacher must be in his inner life.   What are the seals
and marks of his apostleship?   It is, of course, not
possible here to explore the full range of this theme, or
indeed to do more than touch upon certain distinctive
qualities, singling them out from many others which
might equally have been mentioned.   I suggest the
following points.

First, the true preacher will be *a man utterly dedicated
to his work*.   "This one thing I do."   The Christian
ministry opens a door into the most absorbing life-
work under heaven;   and there is something seriously
wrong with the man who, entering it, is not wholly
absorbed.   Unless we are prepared, with joyous and
deliberate abandon, to be mastered, dominated and
controlled by the great task, we ought to thrust it from
us once for all, and not mock Christ with tepid loyalties
and divided interests.   This kind of spiritual concentration is, of course, a totally different thing from the
strained and stubborn austerity which refuses to relax.
It is hardly likely that any preacher will enhance his

efficiency by going from one year's end to another without a holiday or a hobby, as though it were glorifying God to ignore the Master's word, "Come ye yourselves apart, and rest awhile." Equally mistaken is the absorption which consists in shutting oneself off from life, dwelling remote from the common interests of market, street and home, out of touch with the crowding cares and hopes and joys and agonies that mould the lives of men. The condemnation of that attitude is that it is downright inhuman and terribly unlike Jesus. But the fact remains that the servant of the evangel—more than anyone else, more than scientist, artist, composer or man of affairs—must be possessed, heart and mind and soul, by the momentous enterprise that has laid its compulsion upon him.

It would be unnecessary to emphasize this, were it not that slackness is such an insidious peril. This common sin has beggared the rich promise of many a ministry and blunted the cutting edge of its spiritual power. The very conditions of a minister's work—which put into his own hands the control of his time and the ordering of his days—impose a peculiar responsibility. If he fritters time away in idleness, if he squanders in desultory reading of the newspaper and magazine reviews those precious morning hours which ought to be rigorously safeguarded for wrestling with the Word of God, if when Sunday comes he offers to his people sermons shoddy with lack of thought, he damages his troth to Christ and dishonours his high calling. He proves himself to be culpably impercipient of the deep spiritual needs and longings of those whom the great Shepherd has committed to his care. He has never heard the inarticulate crying of the hungry flock: "O refresh us, travelling through this wilderness." He is the hireling who careth not for the sheep.

What right (to put it no higher) have we to speak to the labouring and the heavy-laden, if we are not ourselves as busy as the hardest toiler amongst them? Common decency ought to tell us that to stand in a pulpit on Sunday, and presume to instruct in the things of God men and women who all the week before have been beating us in simple faithfulness to duty, is a mockery and a sham. Rudimentary as this consideration is, it nevertheless calls for emphasis and plain speaking. Beware the professional busy-ness which is but slackness in disguise! The trouble is that we may even succeed in deceiving ourselves. Our diary is crowded. Meetings, discussions, interviews, committees throng the hectic page. We are driven here, there, everywhere by the whirling machinery of good works. We become all things to all men. Laziness? The word, we protest, is not in our vocabulary. Are we not engrossed from morning till night? Do we not conspicuously spend our days under the high pressure of an exacting life? But God, who searches the heart, knows how much of our outward strenuousness is but a rationalization of a latent slackness. What does it all amount to—the whole paraphernalia of good works and religious machinery—if there is lacking the intense concentration on the message which is to deliver men's eyes from tears, their feet from falling, and their souls from death, the lonely wrestling with God at Peniel without which no blessing comes?

"We are seeking," cried Richard Baxter to his brother preachers, "to uphold the world, to save it from the curse of God, to perfect the creation, to attain the ends of Christ's redemption. And are these works to be done with a careless mind or a lazy mind or a lazy hand? O see that this work be done with all your might! Study hard, for the well is deep." It is indeed intolerable to be slack or lethargic in the preparation of a message upon which issues of such incalculable moment hang. What is at stake in our work is the lives of men. Every sermon is to be preached in the knowledge that for someone present it may be now the fulness of the time and the day of salvation. "I take you to record this day," exclaimed Paul, "that I am pure from the blood of all men." Dare we look such words in the face? There was a day when Ezekiel, caught up in the Spirit, heard a voice from heaven crying, "If the watchman see the sword come, and blow not the trumpet, and the people be not warned; if the sword come, and take any person from amongst them, he is taken away in his iniquity; but his blood will I require at the watchman's hand." And as he pondered the vision, suddenly with terrific dramatic force the voice went on: "So thou, O son of man, I have set thee a watchman unto the house of Israel." Age after age, this has been the great prophetic motive. Always the man of God has been the watchman on the

ramparts of the world. Always the preacher of the
Word has known himself to be a sentinel, appointed to
keep vigil over immortal souls. Always the pressure
of the immense responsibility has constrained him to
cry, "Necessity is laid upon me: woe is me, if I preach
not the Gospel!" That is not rhetoric. It is not the
vehement, declamatory talk of the pietist or the fanatic.
It is the plain unemotional declaration of the man who
has grasped the essential issues of his calling. "These
sheep of the Saviour's flock, these blundering, sinning,
suffering, lovable men and women, these I must render
again to the Lord who has given them to me, these I
must offer at the throne in righteousness: else—God
will ask the reason why! Their blood will God require
at the watchman's hand." It is when this ultimate
challenge stabs our conscience that we learn to see
slackness, that ruinous besetting sin of so many a
ministry, in its true colours, and make our vows unto
the Lord against it.

Redemptive work is always costly. There is no
hope of ease for the faithful servant of the Cross. It is
involved in the very nature of his task that he can never
be at the end of it. Not his to evade the burden and
the heat of the day: physical weariness, sickness of
heart and bitter disappointment, the strain of the
passion for souls, all the wear and tear of vicarious
burden-bearing—these he will know in full measure.
He may even find himself wondering sometimes why
he ever accepted a commission in a warfare in which
there is no discharge. He may have moods when a

haunting sense of anticlimax overwhelms him. It is one thing to set out gallantly when the flags are waving and the drums summoning to a new crusade, but it is quite another thing to keep plodding on when the road is difficult and the initial impetus has spent its force and the trumpets of the dawn have ceased to blow. It is one thing to have inspirations: it is another to have tenacity. "My little children," wrote Paul to the Galatians, "of whom I travail in birth again until Christ be formed in you": a swift and startling turn of phrase giving a profoundly moving insight into the price of true Christian ambassadorship. For—

it is by no breath,
Turn of eye, wave of hand, that salvation joins issue with death!—

and if ever a man finds the work of the ministry becoming easily manageable and surmountable, an undemanding vocation without strain or any encumbering load of care, he is to be pitied, not congratulated: for he has so flagrantly lost touch with One whose ministry of reconciliation could be accomplished and fulfilled only through Gethsemane and Calvary. "Without shedding of blood there is no remission of sins." Unless something of the evangelist's life-blood goes into his quest for souls and into the word he brings them from the Lord, the quest remains fruitless and the word devoid of delivering power.

That the ministry should be regarded (as in fact it has sometimes been regarded) as a profession—a career whose main qualifications are a certain amount of organizing ability, tact and culture, the reputation of being a good "mixer" and a shrewd judge of men, some measure of facility of speech, and a decent level of piety—this is shocking and deplorable. No ministry is worth anything which is not first and last and all the time a ministry beneath the Cross. Let a man reckon the cost ere he closes with the call.

There are, indeed, mighty compensations and incomparably precious rewards. You will receive letters which you will treasure all your life as sacred, because they tell gratefully of some vision received, some challenge accepted, some discovery made of the wonderful friendship of Jesus; and when, for one reason or another, your work is taking more out of you than you care to tell, and disappointments are encountered, and the haunting question "What is the use?" stands at your door and knocks, you will thank God at such a time that it is possible by opening the drawer where these letters lie, and reading one or more of them again, to send the low mood flying, and to rally and comfort your soul with a sudden vision of the essential worth and splendour of the task, the amazing privilege of being in it at all, and the magnificence of the faithfulness of God.

The true preacher, then, is a man completely dedicated to the high mission on which he is sent forth. He will be resolute and vigilant, lest any secret slackness should invalidate the message he proclaims. Not that he will obtrude his labours, or take credit from his crowded days, or wish that anyone should know the burden of his toil. Nothing could be further from his thoughts: for he is so piercingly aware that the uttermost of his devotion is a paltry, miserable return for what Christ has done for him. "If there is anything," exclaimed Rabbi Duncan, "in which I would be inclined to contradict my Lord, it would be if I heard Him say, 'Well done, good and faithful servant.'"

II

This first mark of the herald of Christ leads on inevitably to the second. He will be *a man of prayer.* Here again, of course, it is necessary to guard against any suggestion of a double standard—as though the cultivation of the devotional life were a professional obligation limited to the few, and not the manifest duty of all. "A man of prayer"—that must be the ideal, not only of the ordained servants of the Gospel, but of everyone who bears the Christian name. All are here alike, for the New Testament knows nothing of a possession of the Spirit as a priestly monopoly, and the life of devotion is meant to be normal Christianity. The basic reason why a minister must pray is not because he is a minister (that would savour of official piety, always an odious thing), but because he is a poor, needy creature dependent on God's grace.

That is fundamental. But is it not also evident that the weight of his peculiar responsibility must drive him to his knees? If he is taking his work seriously at all, there will be days when Moses' hot outburst to the Lord will echo in his heart: "Wherefore layest Thou the burden of all this people upon me? Have I conceived all this people? Have I begotten them, that Thou shouldst say unto me, Carry them in thy bosom? I am not able to bear all this people alone, because it is too heavy for me." It is out of such a mood of desperate defeat and bankruptcy that there rises, like a bright and morning star, the discovery of prayer's unsearchable riches, its power to steady the staggering soul, to replenish the lost virtue and the nervous energy which the toil of the passion for souls has drained away. Day after day, year after year, you will be expending yourselves, giving out to others. You simply cannot face the strain, except on one condition: you must simultaneously be taking in from God.

Once there was lived upon this earth a life of terrible self-giving, yet of uttermost serenity. Do not we, who grow so hectic often and strained and tired and overburdened, long to share the secret of Christ's peace? It was the secret known to the mountain-tops where He outwatched the stars, to the olive trees in the garden which heard His voice at midnight, to the winds and waves that were His shrine while He communed with God. How shall any man be strong to do Christ's work to-day, with the purposefulness and passion and mastery of life that shine on every page of the Gospels, if he neglects Christ's hidden secret? Chalmers was indeed going to the root of the matter when he declared that most failures in the ministry were due, not to lack of visiting or of study or of organizational activity, but to lack of prayer.

There is more at stake in this than the reinforcing of your spirit or the culture of your private devotions. For whether your congregation be large or small a great part of your task on its behalf lies in the realm of intercession. I do not simply mean asking God to bless your people collectively—though, of course, you will do that—I mean praying for every family, each separate soul, by name. Let me assure you that this suggestion is entirely practicable, whether you have a hundred members or two thousand. Method and system, of course, are necessary; but is there any reason why prayer should not be methodical? Take your Communion Roll. Use it as a directory of intercession. Single out, say, three families each day. Mention each member of these homes by name. Visualize their circumstances. Think of their work, their difficulties, their temptations. Remember very specially any who may have been growing indifferent to religious ordinances and drifting away from the Church. Bear them individually upon your heart to the mercy-seat. From such concrete and particular intercession two results will follow. On the one hand, there will be a blessing for those for whom you pray. On the other hand, there will be revealed to you from time to time, even as you intercede for them, practical ways of helpfulness, new avenues of sympathetic understanding, opportunities of showing to this one or that other something of the kindness of God for Jesus' sake. And when you look into their faces on the Sunday, as you lead their worship and proclaim to them afresh the all-sufficient grace of

Christ, that background of your hidden intercessions, of your pleading for them name by name, will lift your words and wing them with love and ardour and reality. God will not refuse the kindling flame when secret prayer has laid its sacrifice upon the altar. And you will prove in your own experience the truth to which that great soldier of the Cross, Samuel Rutherford, gave expression long ago: "I seldom made an errand to God for another, but I got something for myself."

Is it too much to say that revival in the Church depends upon the prayer-life of its ministers? Too often we take for granted that here at least all is well. But still to-day, as when the winds of Pentecost stirred the world, the first essential is the broken spirit and the contrite heart of those who preach the Word, the sense of dreadful inadequacy driving every apostle to his knees. To realize, face to face with the task, that it is hopeless trying to go on unless higher hands take hold of you; to know the feeling of utter incapacity which creates a trust that is vital just because it is desperate; to cry to God out of that depth of humiliation every day you live—this is to learn the secret of the apostles, whose very weakness was turned through the alchemy of prayer into their strongest asset, whose human inadequacy itself became the vehicle of the conquering might of Christ. "We have this treasure in earthen vessels, to show that the excellency of the power is of God, and not of us." It is when a man strikes rock-bottom in his sense of nothingness that he suddenly finds he has struck the Rock of ages. Then his whole ministry is supernaturalized, and through him the Spirit can act with power. "In Love's service," says the Angel in Thornton Wilder's play, "only the wounded soldiers can serve." And only those who have been wounded in the region of their human confidence, whose self-sufficiency has been shattered into supplication, only they can be the healers of this ailing world. Be sure of this, that if men are to be blessed by your ministry, prayer must be its alpha and its omega. "Our sufficiency is of God."

III

This brings us to the third characteristic note of the preacher's inner life. He will be *a man marked by a great humility of heart*. Nowhere surely are pride and self-importance and conscious striving after effect more incongruous and unpardonable than in the servant of the Cross. Yet pride would not be the basic sin it is, if it did not possess this demonic quality, that precisely where you would expect to find it lying dead for ever, there it reappears, insinuating itself in even subtler guise. "The final human pretension," Reinhold Niebuhr has reminded us, "is made most successfully under the aegis of a religion which has overcome human pretension in principle." "I am an apostle," wrote Paul to the Romans; "I magnify mine office"—for it is right to think greatly of a calling so momentous in its issues for the Kingdom of Christ and the souls of men. But that there can be a false magnifying of the

ministerial office, Paul himself reminds us trenchantly
in another passage. Read the fourth chapter of First
Corinthians, and you will see the apostle's irony flashing like a rapier against the self-display, the acceptance
of adulation, and all the stratagems of a latent egotism
which too often have intruded themselves into tne
service of the Lord. Two hundred years ago, William
Law in his *Serious Call* laid it down flatly that to serve
Christ self-importantly is to be both a thief and a liar:
"It has the guilt of stealing, as it gives to ourselves
those things which belong only to God; and it has the
guilt of lying, as it is the denying the truth of our state,
and pretending to be something that we are not."

This, certainly, is true Biblical teaching. "Who
maketh thee to differ from another? What hast thou
that thou didst not receive? Why dost thou glory, as if
thou hadst not received it?" Imagine a poor dauber
setting his amateurish efforts alongside a Raphael or a
Titian: "Yes, it is rather good, that work of mine!"
What are our best words for Christ compared with the
Christ of whom we speak? What is our uttermost of
devotion in the presence of that blazing holiness?
"All our righteousnesses are as filthy rags," all our
anxious concern "Did I preach well to-day?" is dust
and ashes in the presence of the Cross: that every
mouth may be stopped before God.

Observe that there are three contributory factors
here. The first we have noted already. It is the
magnitude of the task. To build something of the
New Jerusalem in your own parish and field of labour,

to fight for social justice and the Christian ethic in the
wider community, to carry upon your heart the sorrows
and shames and sins of the souls committed to your
care, to be amongst them as a witness and a herald,
"to present" (as Paul put it) "every man perfect in
Christ Jesus"—could you conceive any task more
humbling in its appalling responsibility? There is a
great sermon of John Donne's, delivered in the year
1624, in which he sets forth his conception of the awful
burden on the preacher's heart. "What Sea," cries
Donne, "could furnish mine eyes with teares enough
to poure out, if I should think, that of all this congregation, which lookes me in the face now, I should not
meet one at the Resurrection, at the right hand of
God! When at any midnight I hear a bell toll from
this steeple, must not I say to my selfe, what have I
done at any time for the instructing or rectifying of
that man's Conscience, who lieth there now ready to
deliver up his own account and my account to Almighty God?" Is it to be wondered at that many a
man of God besides Elijah and Jeremiah has tried to
run away from a commission so crushing and intolerable? Nothing but the grace of God can hold you to
it. The magnitude of the task is the first element in
evangelical humility.

The second is the unworthiness of the preacher.
Who are we to expound categorically the mysteries of
God and the soul? Our best insights are so frag-
mentary, our ignorance so abysmal. Never forget that
in your congregation there will be those who had been

"born again" before you were born at all. You will
be preaching to some who will always be "further ben"
in the deep things of God than yourself. Must not
that reflection replace false confidence with modesty?
But ignorance and finitude are not, of course, the sum
total of our unworthiness. "Woe is me! for I am undone; because I am a man of unclean lips: mine eyes
have seen the King." "Only once," wrote Dr. Alexander Whyte, "did God choose a completely sinless
preacher." Our doom it is that with no atom of
personal merit or deserving, with nothing indeed but
broken contrition and the shame of sin's radical corruption, we have to tell of Jesus and His love. Let the
preacher, charged to mediate the word of God to men,
pause ere he mount the pulpit-steps and breathe the
secret prayer, "God be merciful to me a sinner."
There will be days when the sense of personal unworthiness smites and shatters us, until we cry "My
God, why hast Thou forsaken me?" It is then, by
some miracle of divine lovingkindness, at such a
moment of desolation, that there comes the angel,
touching a man's lips with a live coal from the altar
of God.

There is a third reason for the humility which will
always mark the servant of the evangel. This is the
fact that anything his work may achieve is God's doing,
not his own. If visible results attend his ministry, if
souls are brought out of darkness into light, if the
faithful are strengthened and the apathetic awakened
and the spiritually dead resurrected (and, mark you,

unless he is aiming at these things he has no right to
be in the ministry at all), if success in this deep sense
is granted, he will not seek to depreciate it or ignore it,
for that would be dangerously like the sin against the
Holy Ghost: but equally he will not take to himself
one grain of credit for it, for it is the doing of the Lord
alone. It is only God who can take the five loaves and
the two fishes—our paltry, scanty offering—and make
it a banquet for the hungry souls of men. Moreover,
preaching (as we saw in a previous lecture) is essentially
worship, and in worship all human glorying is excluded,
for the God whom we adore fills the whole horizon,
and our mood is that of prostrate Abraham: "Behold
now, I have taken upon me to speak unto the Lord,
which am but dust and ashes." Spurgeon in one place
describes the clergyman who says, "When I was
preaching at such-and-such a place, fifteen persons
came into the vestry at the close of the service, and
thanked me for the sermon I had preached." And
Spurgeon, unable to restrain himself, lets fly furiously
at the complacent creature: "You and your blessed
sermon be hanged! Take not to yourself the honour
which belongeth unto God only."

> All we can do is nothing worth, unless God blesses the deed;
> Vainly we hope for the harvest-tide, till God gives life to
> the seed.

Here, in the knowledge that the human agent is
nothing—*vox et praeterea nihil*—is the final source of
the preacher's humility of heart. He will rejoice whenever another soul, through his ministry, stumbles upon

the crowning revelation and breaks loose from its fetters and enters the Kingdom; but he will give God the glory. Flesh and blood have not revealed it, but only the Father in heaven.

IV

In the light of what has just been said, the fourth mark of the true preacher, to which we now pass, may appear at first sight paradoxical. He will be *a man of authority*. It is quite mistaken to suppose that humility excludes conviction. G. K. Chesterton once penned some wise words about what he called "the dislocation of humility." "What we suffer from to-day is humility in the wrong place. Modesty has moved from the organ of ambition. Modesty has settled upon the organ of conviction; where it was never meant to be. A man was meant to be doubtful about himself, but undoubting about the truth; this has been exactly reversed. We are on the road to producing a race of men too mentally modest to believe in the multiplication table." Humble and self-forgetting we must be always, but diffident and apologetic about the Gospel never.

When D. L. Moody first carried his evangelism into one of our great University centres, there was some initial opposition. His first meeting was persistently interrupted, punctuated with scoffing epithets. At last Moody broke out. "You jeered at the hymns," he exclaimed, "and I said nothing. You jeered at the prayers and I said nothing. But now you jeer at the Word of God. I would as soon play *with forked lightning*!" Surely the diffidence and lack of assurance which would be appropriate enough in the propagating of private theories or the giving of human advice become ludicrous and nauseating in the proclamation of a Word so swift and powerful and tremendous. "It is not God's ordinary way," cries John Donne, "to be whispering of secrets. For Publication of Himselfe He hath constituted a Church. And in this Church, His Ordinance is Ordinance indeed; His Ordinance of preaching batters the soule, and by that breach, the Spirit enters; His Ministers are an Earthquake, and shake an earthly soule; they are the sonnes of thunder, and scatter a cloudy conscience."

The very terms describing the preacher's function —herald, ambassador—manifestly connote authority. Far too often the pulpit has been deferential and apologetic when it ought to have been prophetic and trumpet-toned. It has wasted time balancing probabilities and discussing opinions and erecting interrogation-marks, when it ought to have been ringing out the note of unabashed, triumphant affirmation—"The mouth of the Lord hath spoken it!"

It is significant that when the vision of the glory of God struck Ezekiel prostrate to the ground, the first words that shattered the silence were "Son of man, stand upon thy feet, and I will speak unto thee." God wants no grovelling, faint-hearted creatures for His ambassadors: He wants men who, having communed

with heaven, can never be intimidated by the world.
You will remember how the same note sounds again
in Paul's account of his conversion. "Who art Thou,
Lord?" "I am Jesus whom thou persecutest. But
rise, and stand upon thy feet: for I have appeared unto
thee for this purpose, to make thee a minister." It is
always thus in every age the ministers of the living
Christ are made—the crushing, paralysing sense of
abject worthlessness, the self-esteem broken and rolled
in the dust, and then a man rising to his full stature as
God's commissioned messenger. "Chief of sinners,"
"least of all saints"—such was Paul's self-estimate ;
yet with what royal, unqualified authority he proclaimed the word and the will of the Lord!

The Christian preacher is the bondslave of Christ
and the servant of all: but let him not confound such
apostolic servitude with spiritual servility. The Gospel
is not servile: it is "mighty through God to the pulling
down of strongholds." Dr. G. L. Prestige, in his
biography of the late Bishop Gore, has described a
sermon Gore preached before the University of Oxford,
in which he sought to distinguish between true humility
and false deference. "Some who heard it long recalled
the trumpet tones and accompanying snorts of derision
with which he quoted the *Magnificat*, interspersing
each passage with contemptuous cries of 'Servile?'"
"Stand upon thy feet," said the voice to Saul of Tarsus,
"for I will make thee a minister, *delivering thee from
the people*": for to have stood before Christ is to be
clothed with an authority that defies subservience and

fears no face of man. To quote Donne again—"So
the Apostles proceeded; when they came in their
peregrination to a new State, to a new Court, to Rome
it selfe, they did not enquire, how stands the Emperour
affected to Christ, and to the preaching of His Gospel?
This was not their way; They only considered who
sent them; Christ Jesus: And what they brought;
salvation to every soul." This is the note that modern
preaching must recapture. For this is no time for
Christ's accredited servants to be soft-pedalling their
distinctive message; no time for that peculiarly un-
pleasant form of servility which regards it as a feather
in the Church's cap if some scientist or philosopher or
Brains Trust specialist speaks approvingly and patronizingly of our holy religion; no time to be watering
down the radical and challenging content of the
Christian faith to suit the taste of any vague indeter-
minate humanism that boggles at the supernatural.
We shall never do Christ's work to-day unless—like
our Master—we dare to speak with authority, and
not as the scribes.

But whence comes this authority? It springs, first,
from the fact that it is God's Word, not our own, that
we proclaim. When that noble ambassador of Christ,
Temple Gairdner of Cairo (whose life-story is one of
the classics of missionary biography), was an under-
graduate, he took some share in student meetings
organized by one of the religious societies in the
University. "Do I speak at a meeting?" he wrote in
a letter to a friend, "I am asked, 'Are you better than

those here, that you speak to them?' Nay, but Christ
is better—I do not speak of myself but of Him." It
is this that redeems our stammering lips from confusion, and gives the veriest sinner words that ring like
iron and shine like flame. "You have not chosen Me,"
says Jesus—that would be too flimsy and fortuitous
to be a basis for apostleship—"but I have chosen you":
that rallies all the latent courage of the soul. It is "in
Christ's stead," declared St. Paul, that we who in
ourselves are fallible and sinful creatures announce the
Gospel of reconciliation; and the preacher across
whose consciousness that thrilling word—"in Christ's
stead"—has pealed needs no other apostolic succession
to invest him with the insignia of authority. He is not
diffidently offering men the dubious results of his
private speculation: he is standing on his feet to
deliver to them, in the name of the King of kings, a
word that cannot return void. He preaches as if the
Lord God omnipotent were there at his right hand:
as indeed God is. The keynote of his preaching is not
"Thus I think": it is "Thus saith the Lord." The
late Sir George Adam Smith has described the early
years of Dr. Alexander Whyte's ministry in St. George's,
Edinburgh, and the great preacher's influence on the
student community in particular, to which at that time
Smith himself belonged. "I remember how one of us
coming out of church one day said: 'Well, till hearing
Whyte I never realised that paradox of St. Paul, *I . . .
yet not I.*' There was the natural man himself, the
strong, gifted, ardent personality with his own features,

accents and styles, and his own experiences, all of which came home to our hearts, but it was the Spirit of the Lord which we felt pouring through him." That penetrating analysis goes right to the roots of the secret of true preaching. "I—yet not I, but Christ!" Not mine the witness, not mine the cry and beseeching, not over my poor lips but out from the depths of the eternal breaks the word that is to convict and save. I plead with men, yet not I: Christ pleadeth in me. In Christ, God goes forth in action through the Spirit. "He that hath ears to hear, let him hear "

There is a second, subsidiary source of the preacher's authority. This is the testimony of the Christian centuries behind him and of the universal Church around him. Not as an isolated, lonely figure, intruding oddly upon the contemporary scene, does he stand in his pulpit to-day. What matter though his sphere of labour be thankless and obscure, and his own gifts and talents meagre and unimpressive? Behind him stand Spurgeon and Liddon and Newman and Chalmers and Baxter and Jeremy Taylor and Latimer and Luther and Francis and Augustine and Chrysostom and Paul. Those who belittle the vocation of the preacher prove the poverty of their own historic imagination: for behind every pulpit from which the Word is faithfully proclaimed to-day there stretches the august pageant of the gathering ages. It is an immensely thrilling experience to know, when you tell men of Christ the Lord, that your poor words are backed and reinforced by the witness of two thousand years. Indeed, the very indestructibility of the Church out of whose bosom you speak, its survival of desperate vicissitudes, its defiance of the gates of hell—this is itself impressive proof of the eternal significance of your ministry and vocation. If ever you feel lonely in your task—and there will be days when crushing loneliness besets you —remember who are your kith and kin, Columba and Xavier and Savonarola and Knox and Wesley and all the multitude who in every generation have preached the identical Christ whom you preach to-day, one Lord, one faith, one baptism, one Cross, one victory, one mercy-seat, one building not made with hands, eternal in the heavens. Nor need you turn your gaze to the past only. Lift up your eyes, and look around you; and realize that, while you stand solitary in your pulpit, yonder—at that very moment—beyond the walls of your church and out to earth's remotest bounds a great host of witnesses are publishing the same tidings which you now bear upon your heart. So the littleness and the inadequacy of the individual preacher are caught up into the context of historic Christianity; and his message rings, not with the dogmatism of a self-assured complacency, but with the authoritative testimony of a great cloud of witnesses, the glorious company of the apostles, the goodly fellowship of the prophets, the noble army of martyrs, and the holy Church throughout all the world.

Yet even this is not enough. The preacher proclaims God's word, not his own; and he proclaims it out of the midst of the Christian fellowship. But a third factor is needful to vest him in the authority of a true ambassador. He must possess the word—or rather, he must be possessed by it—as a living, personal experience. Why is it that two men, enunciating the very same truths, may differ utterly in results achieved? The one declares the salvation of Christ, and little or nothing happens. The other, using almost the identical words, declares the same salvation, and chords are set vibrating in a hundred hearts. It is in the realm of personal experience that the difference lies. There were certain Jewish exorcists, the writer of the Book of Acts narrates, who tried to do the works of God and cast out evil spirits by using the formula, "I adjure you by Jesus whom Paul preacheth." As if miracles could be wrought in the name of someone else's Christ! Are we to tell men to-day of a Christ whom the apostles preached, or Luther, or the Wesleys, or our own immediate fathers in the faith? It is not surprising that the sons of Sceva in the Book of Acts, adjuring their congregation by Jesus whom Paul preached, met the blunt retort—"Jesus we know, and Paul we know, but who are ye?" You may preach Paul's Christ or Calvin's Christ, and not break a single shackle of sin or bind up one broken heart. There is not authority enough in second-hand religion to rouse the listless and set the captives free. But how different it is when, like the apostle, the twentieth-century preacher can declare "my Gospel," when he is manifestly building not on rumour and hearsay but on the proved facts of his own experience, and when those hearkening to his word are constrained to say—"There is a man who has been with Jesus!"

This, of course, is not to say that you are to keep talking about your own soul, or dragging your secret experiences into the light. Emphatically not: such self-exposure in the pulpit is apt to make all decent men and women squirm, and the note of autobiography soon becomes mawkish and insufferable. "Stand out of the way," men feel like saying to such a preacher, "and let us through to Jesus!" But if self-obtrusion is to be discountenanced, the fact remains that the only sermon the world wants to hear is one that throbs with the vitality of first-hand knowledge and experience. This alone carries authority and conviction. This leaves men saying, "God spoke to us to-day."

Therefore it is essential that, right on to the very end of his ministry, the preacher's own vision of God in Christ should be a growing and expanding thing. No doubt the last sermon that you ever preach on earth will contain the same Gospel with which you first launched out on the day of your ordination. Yet surely there will be a difference. For all along the road, God will have been speaking to you, enlarging your experience with new disclosures of His grace. And if, as we have seen, authority is born of personal apprehension of the truth, it is well to remember that such apprehension is never final: it is always, as Hosea expressed it, a "following on to know the Lord." God asks no man to face to-day in the strength of yesterday's grace, or to hoard for his sustenance to-morrow manna gathered to-day. "I will make thee a minister and a witness," said the risen Christ to Saul of Tarsus, "both of these things which thou hast seen, and of those things in the which I will appear unto thee": for beyond the Damascus vision there was a whole world of spiritual knowledge waiting to be explored, and when he lay in prison near the end he was reaching out to know Christ better still in the power of His Resurrection and the fellowship of His sufferings. However long your ministry, there need be no danger of the blight of staleness and stagnation, if your personal experience of Christ is growing all the time. Here is the ultimate secret of authoritative preaching—a first-hand knowledge, never inert and static, never dependent merely on remembered episodes, shining and decisive God-encounters long ago, but always dynamic and developing, always with insight added to insight, and wonder piled on wonder, from the moment when you first gird on your armour for the fray, until the last sermon is preached and the long campaign is over and your work on earth is done.

v

We have been inquiring into the nature of the preacher's inner life. We have distinguished certain vital marks of his apostleship. There are others, too numerous to mention here. Let it suffice to call attention to one final, indispensable quality. He will be *a man on fire for Christ*.

God help the preacher who tries to ply this work with no overpowering sense of its urgency! When you remember, as you stand in your pulpit, that some around you there have been lifting you to God, to gird your soul with strength and your words with the authority of Jesus; that never a congregation gathers, but some expectant souls are present, hoping and hungering for the open heavens and the vision of the Lord; that always there are some trembling on the verge of spiritual decision, so that for them this very service might be the hour of life's supreme encounter; that every one of those into whose faces you look is so infinitely precious that for their sakes Christ was willing to endure the Cross and despise the shame—when you reflect on this, must not your spirit catch fire, and all listlessness and formality be burned up in the glow of the evangel? Here is the source of authentic inspiration, "the demon of preaching," as it is sometimes called. When all is said and done, the supreme need of the Church is the same in the twentieth century as in the first: it is men on fire for Christ.

I beg you not to commit the fearful blunder of damping down that flame. It is, of course, understandable and right that you who are going out into the ministry should distrust, and set your faces against, the spurious fervour which notoriously brings discredit on the faith. But the pity is that there are preachers so frightened of this taint that they have actually done violence to the flame Christ has kindled within them, choosing deliberately an attitude of cool and imperturb-